Revelation, a Balanced View

By Ian Grant Spong

© 2020 by Ian Grant Spong

Contents

Introduction

What is Revelation all about? What are the mysterious creatures and other symbols supposed to mean? This is a series for personal and group Bible Studies discovering the real secrets in the book of Revelation. Most of the quotes are from the Public Domain King James Bible, not because I superstitiously believe it is more accurate, which it is not, but because copyright rules do not allow extensive quotation of most modern translations.

Being brought up on the KJV when it was popular, I learned to read the words in modern English, for instance, pronouncing things like "readeth" as "reads," "hath" as "has," "saith" as "says" and so on. May I challenge you to do the same. If you prefer another translation, may I suggest simply placing it in front of you as you follow along in this study.

What does attempting a balanced view mean? There are four major views of the book of Revelation: Preterist, Historicist, Futurist and Symbolic (Spiritual). The view that most fits the genre is the symbolic view, yet it also allows consideration of the other views.

Preterism is that view that all or most of the prophecies were fulfilled pre-Constantine, mostly around the fall of Jerusalem.

Historicism is that view that most of the prophecies are fulfilled throughout history from the legalization of Christianity under Constantine and forward. Futurism sees most of the prophetic events as occurring just before the return of Christ and beyond.

The spiritual or symbolic view recognizes that apocalyptic literature is a symbolic genre. So, it makes the most sense, and has the advantage of being able to include relevant aspects of the other three views, thus giving a balance. It is this balance that we will attempt to strike as we study Revelation together.

The reader may also be aware that many wacky and outlandish views of Revelation exist. We will attempt to avoid the absurd extremes and instead seek a balance of wisdom and understanding that the Holy Spirit has given to the Church throughout Christian history. May the Lord bless us as we contemplate these mysteries together.

Revelation 1 - Whose Revelation

Though we are introduced to a cast of mysterious characters, the book tells us in the first few words that it is by and about Jesus. We see Him in all His current glory. Let's begin in chapter 1.

Revelation 1:1-2 The Revelation of Jesus Christ, which God gave unto him, to shew unto his servants things which must shortly come to pass; and he sent and signified it by his angel unto his servant John: Who bare record of the word of God, and of the testimony of Jesus Christ, and of all things that he saw.

Is this the revealing of the meaning of the 4 horses, 7 seals, 666, 1000 years, 144 thousand, Armageddon, Babylon, Beast, Gog, Magog, Harlot, Lampstands, Olive Trees, and Trumpets? The first sentence gives us the purpose of the book. It is NOT primarily the revelation of such symbols, it is primarily the revelation or UNVEILING OF a person. Both meanings (*ABOUT* and *BY* Jesus) are relevant in a sentence which is perhaps purposefully ambiguous in both English and Greek. In the same manner, it is also the TESTIMONY about and by that same person, Jesus Christ.

Revelation 1:3 Blessed is he that readeth, and they that hear the words of this prophecy, and keep those things which are written therein: for the time is at hand.

It is easy to dismiss Revelation as too mysterious to understand, or not central to Christian teaching. However, those who do, also dismiss the promised blessing for reading the book. Let's not miss that blessing, and keep reading together.

Revelation 1:4-6 John to the seven churches which are in Asia: Grace be unto you, and peace, from him which is, and which was, and which is to come; and from the seven Spirits which are before his throne; And from Jesus Christ, who is the faithful witness, and the first begotten of the dead, and the prince of the kings of the earth. Unto him that loved us, and washed us from our sins in his own blood, And hath made us kings and priests unto God and his Father; to him be glory and dominion for ever and ever. Amen.

Whether the seven spirits are the seven angels of the seven churches or the seven-fold Holy Spirit is a question among theologians. Revelation is a letter addressed to seven churches in the once Greek speaking geographical area of modern day western

Turkey. The ancient style of epistle is obvious. It is also in another genre, called the apocalyptic genre, which we will come to learn more about.

Revelation 1:7 Behold, he cometh with clouds; and every eye shall see him, and they also which pierced him: and all kindreds of the earth shall wail because of him. Even so, Amen.

Next we notice that at His return, Jesus will be visible, not invisible. This was also attested to at the ascension of Jesus. *"Men of Galilee," they said, "why are you standing here staring into heaven? Jesus has been taken from you into heaven, but someday he will return from heaven in the same way you saw him go!"* (Acts 1:11 NLT) The theory of a secret return is a departure from this testimony.

Revelation 1:8 I am Alpha and Omega, the beginning and the ending, saith the Lord [God], which is, and which was, and which is to come, the Almighty.

The Word "God" [in square brackets] is in the original Greek and most modern translations include it here. The words "the beginning and the ending" are from Revelation 22:13. God the Father and later God the Son, are both described as alpha and omega. Though this prophecy describes the dragon and the beast, we know that the end will be the same as the beginning, God reigns and all false gods are temporary. The Almighty means the ruler of all.

Revelation 1:9 I John, who also am your brother, and companion in tribulation, and in the kingdom and patience of Jesus Christ, was in the isle that is called Patmos, for the word of God, and for the testimony of Jesus Christ.

Independent evidence suggests that John was a prisoner on Patmos.

Revelation 1:10 I was in the Spirit on the Lord's day, and heard behind me a great voice, as of a trumpet,

Ancient church fathers separated the Sabbath from the Lord's Day. The 7th day remembered creation. The 1st day remembered the Resurrection and became a weekly mini Easter Sunday. It seems then, that John spent all Sunday in worship accompanied by a vision.

Revelation 1:11 Saying, I am Alpha and Omega, the first and the last: and, What thou seest, write in a book, and send it unto the seven churches which are in Asia; unto Ephesus, and unto Smyrna, and unto

Pergamos, and unto Thyatira, and unto Sardis, and unto Philadelphia, and unto Laodicea.

This Sunday experience was to be preserved in writing and as we shall see, though based upon the seven churches, it was intended for the edification of a much wider audience.

Revelation 1:12-13 And I turned to see the voice that spake with me. And being turned, I saw seven golden candlesticks; And in the midst of the seven candlesticks one like unto the Son of man, clothed with a garment down to the foot, and girt about the paps with a golden girdle.

The Old Testament church was pictured in one unified candlestick with 7 branches, the menorah (Exodus 25:31-32; Zechariah 4:2-11). The New Testament church is pictured in seven individual candlesticks, not one unified whole. Who is in the midst of the 7 churches? Is it Jesus?

Revelation 1:14-15 His head and his hairs were white like wool, as white as snow; and his eyes were as a flame of fire; And his feet like unto fine brass, as if they burned in a furnace; and his voice as the sound of many waters.

Reminiscent of the vision seen on the mount of transfiguration (Matthew 17:2), is a similar vision of Jesus' present glory. We may as well be honest and upright in prayer. Jesus' piercing eyes see right through any pretense we might muster.

Revelation 1:16 And he had in his right hand seven stars: and out of his mouth went a sharp twoedged sword: and his countenance was as the sun shineth in his strength.

The word of God which goes forth from Jesus' mouth is like a two edged sword (Hebrews 4:12).

Revelation 1:17-18 And when I saw him, I fell at his feet as dead. And he laid his right hand upon me, saying unto me, Fear not; I am the first and the last: I am he that liveth, and was dead; and, behold, I am alive for evermore, Amen; and have the keys of hell and of death.

Like Daniel (10:8-9), John, who was Jesus' closest companion, was so overwhelmed that he fell upon seeing the resurrected Christ.

Revelation 1:19 Write the things which thou hast seen, and the things which are, and the things which shall be hereafter;

No time frame is given as to the exact timing of these events to come. It is perhaps deliberately vague, neither exclusively supporting a preterist (already past) nor a futurist (yet future) view.

Revelation 1:20 The mystery of the seven stars which thou sawest in my right hand, and the seven golden candlesticks. The seven stars are the angels of the seven churches: and the seven candlesticks which thou sawest are the seven churches.

It is clear who the seven candlesticks are. The seven angels are either heavenly or human "messengers," perhaps bishops or presbyters. Heavenly angels do not need letters, though letters can be symbolic of heaven's marching orders.

Revelation 2 - 7 Churches

Let's move into an exciting lesson about the churches that we attend, mirrored in seven ancient churches.

Ephesus

Revelation 2:1-3 "To the angel of the church of Ephesus write, 'These things says He who holds the seven stars in His right hand, who walks in the midst of the seven golden lampstands: 2 I know your works, your labor, your patience, and that you cannot bear those who are evil. And you have tested those who say they are apostles and are not, and have found them liars; 3 and you have persevered and have patience, and have labored for My name's sake and have not become weary.

Caesar's son was pictured as surrounded by seven stars, yet Jesus holds them in His hand. This same powerful Jesus, who controls the universe, walks among the churches. Ephesus is commended for diligence, perseverance, intolerance of evil people and fraudulent apostles. Many of today's churches could not be given the same praise.

Revelation 2:4-5 Nevertheless I have this against you, that you have left your first love. 5 Remember therefore from where you have fallen; repent and do the first works, or else I will come to you quickly and remove your lampstand from its place—unless you repent.

Many of our modern churches have also left their first love. In defining the greatest commandment (Matthew 22:36-40; Mark 12:28-34; Luke 10:25-28), Jesus was very specific as to which was the first, love of God.

A major fault of the so-called "social gospel" can highlight the love of our neighbor and overlook the love of God. This causes an upside down approach to worship, whereby the God-breathed Word of Holy Scripture is placed second to the cultural dictates of our neighbors. Many believed in Jesus but would not confess Him because of fear they would be put out of the synagogue. We too have "loved the praise of men more than the praise of God." (John 12:43)

The ancient church of Ephesus is no more, having lost its place. Today, the sin of Ephesus continues, because many have also left their first love, the love of God and obedience to His written instructions. Through Ephesus, we are reminded to "do the first works" and that love involves action. Where have we failed to love God with all our hearts, souls, strength and minds? What works have we neglected to do?

Revelation 2:6 But this you have, that you hate the deeds of the Nicolaitans, which I also hate.

Who were the Nicolaitans? Nicolaism was one of many ancient heresies. Moderns may be shocked that "inclusivity" has boundaries and does not include apostates. Early church fathers wrote of various licentious errors named for the deacon Nicolas (Acts 6:5). Whether he was to blame or not is uncertain. The context shows that these false ideas, which had infiltrated some churches, were not tolerated in Ephesus.

Revelation 2:7 He who has an ear, let him hear what the Spirit says to the churches. To him who overcomes I will give to eat from the tree of life, which is in the midst of the Paradise of God.

All of us, in every age and place are encouraged to heed this instruction, penned by a mere man in an ancient cultural context, yet inspired by the Holy Spirit with universal symbolism. We are also encouraged to overcome the worldly influence that had crept into 5 of the 7 churches. Why? Because, most of our churches today are also too worldly.

Can salvation come even in very heretical modern churches? The same principle applies today: "to him who overcomes." Overcoming may be more difficult in some church situations than others, but the hope of salvation exists even in churches that are very corrupt.

Smyrna

Revelation 2:8 And unto the angel of the church in Smyrna write; These things saith the first and the last, which was dead, and is alive;

Smyrna is modern Izmir, Turkey. The city was dead for 300 years and came back to life. This is only one of two churches not told to repent.

Revelation 2:9 I know thy works, and tribulation, and poverty, (but thou art rich) and I know the blasphemy of them which say they are Jews, and are not, but are the synagogue of Satan.

Their tribulation and poverty were caused by persecution. Could we lose everything and remain rich in faith (James 2:5)? Contrast this with wealthy Laodicean believers who are in spiritual reality poor. Christians of Smyrna were oppressed by the large Jewish population.

Revelation 2:10 Fear none of those things which thou shalt suffer: behold, the devil shall cast some of you into prison, that ye may be tried; and ye shall have tribulation ten days: be thou faithful unto death, and I will give thee a crown of life.

The encouragement not to be fearful is to work through our anxieties and not allow ourselves to be bullied into silence and to remain faithful even if it means death. Today, one in nine Christians are persecuted for their faith, most severely across north Africa and Asia, where many still experience martyrdom.

Revelation 2:11 He that hath an ear, let him hear what the Spirit saith unto the churches; He that overcometh shall not be hurt of the second death.

Again we are reminded that, whether this is a historic prophecy fulfilled in ten periods of Roman persecution, awaiting a future fulfillment, or symbolic of all persecution experienced down through the ages, this is still relevant for us and we should listen. Even in a church that receives the Spirit's approval, the call remains to be an overcomer.

Pergamos

Revelation 2:12 And to the angel of the church in Pergamos write; These things saith he which hath the sharp sword with two edges;

Pergamos was famous for its large library, emperor worship and worship of other gods. The two edged sword is a loving scalpel removing the cancer of sin.

Revelation 2:13 I know thy works, and where thou dwellest, even where Satan's seat is: and thou holdest fast my name, and hast not denied my faith, even in those days wherein Antipas was my faithful martyr, who was slain among you, where Satan dwelleth.

Satan's throne and martyrdom seem to go hand-in-hand, where the worship of the serpent god Æsculapius was a reminder of Satan.

Revelation 2:14 But I have a few things against thee, because thou hast there them that hold the doctrine of Balaam, who taught Balac to cast a stumblingblock before the children of Israel, to eat things sacrificed unto idols, and to commit fornication.

Balaam was known for setting a honey trap, enticing Israel to fornication so that God would curse them. There are modern equivalents to eating meat sacrificed to idols. In principle, it involves going along with any societal evil, so that neighbors would not ostracize us or that we would lose business.

Revelation 2:15 So hast thou also them that hold the doctrine of the Nicolaitanes, which thing I hate.

The doctrine of the Nicolaitans is pictured in many kinds of sexual sin today.

Revelation 2:16 Repent; or else I will come unto thee quickly, and will fight against them with the sword of my mouth.

What is the answer to our many modern sexual sins? The Word of God and repentance!

Revelation 2:17 He that hath an ear, let him hear what the Spirit saith unto the churches; To him that overcometh will I give to eat of the hidden manna, and will give him a white stone, and in the stone a new name written, which no man knoweth saving he that receiveth it.

Again, the Spirit encourages all to hear and be overcomers. The hidden manna is symbolic of the bread of life. The white stone may refer to a pass admitting the holder to a feast.

Thyatira

Revelation 2:18 And unto the angel of the church in Thyatira write; These things saith the Son of God, who hath his eyes like unto a flame of fire, and his feet are like fine brass;

Also described in 1:14, Jesus' bright and shining eyes are explained in 2:23 as searching our innermost desires and thoughts.

Revelation 2:19 I know thy works, and charity, and service, and faith, and thy patience, and thy works; and the last to be more than the first.

This is a church with a living faith evidenced by their good works. They have also grown doing better than at first. How many of our churches could Jesus say that to?

Revelation 2:20 Notwithstanding I have a few things against thee, because thou sufferest that woman Jezebel, which calleth herself a prophetess, to teach and to seduce my servants to commit fornication, and to eat things sacrificed unto idols.

They were led astray by a woman given the same name as the wife of Israel's most corrupt king Ahab, indicating her true character, which was marked by sexual sin and compromise with idolatry.

Revelation 2:21 And I gave her space to repent of her fornication; and she repented not.

Judgment is not always immediate upon apostate bishops and false prophets of the church. Sometimes God gives time to repent.

Revelation 2:22 Behold, I will cast her into a bed, and them that commit adultery with her into great tribulation, except they repent of their deeds.

The adultery may have been literal and spiritual. Idolatry is disloyalty to God, as adultery is disloyalty to a spouse. Modern Jezebel's should shudder at their certain punishment unless they repent.

Revelation 2:23 And I will kill her children with death; and all the churches shall know that I am he which searcheth the reins and hearts: and I will give unto every one of you according to your works.

Calamity can be from persecution or natural forces (Ecclesiastes 9:11; Luke 13:1-3), or as punishment from God as is this warning to Jezebel.

Revelation 2:24 But unto you I say, and unto the rest in Thyatira, as many as have not this doctrine, and which have not known the depths of Satan, as they speak; I will put upon you none other burden.

Some remain faithful, even in churches led by very sinful people.

Revelation 2:25 But that which ye have already hold fast till I come.

God may inspire us to continue attending even an apostate church, as a witness. If so, we are encouraged to hold fast to the Word of God, confessing the faith once for all delivered to the saints (Jude 3). Hold fast to the teachings (2 Thessalonians 2:15), our confession (Hebrews 4:14; 10:23), what is good (1 Thessalonians 5:21), to the word (1 Corinthians 15:2).

Revelation 2:26 And he that overcometh, and keepeth my works unto the end, to him will I give power over the nations:

Again, overcoming is a theme, and contrary to dead faith without works, good works are evidence of a living faith.

Revelation 2:27 And he shall rule them with a rod of iron; as the vessels of a potter shall they be broken to shivers: even as I received of my Father.

Modern Christians are not used to the tough love of Jesus. We prefer a soft, namby pamby

Jesus. Yet, that is not the reality. Unlike that Jezebel, Jesus is tough on sin.

Revelation 2:28 And I will give him the morning star.

The last star of the morning is the planet Venus. The faithful will be first in line after the darkness of this age is past, when the new day dawns of world peace. Jesus is that morning star, and He will gladly give Himself to the faithful remnant (Revelation 22:16).

Revelation 2:29 He that hath an ear, let him hear what the Spirit saith unto the churches.

These messages to the seven churches are for all of us. Let us hear!

We have covered the conditions within four ancient churches. Here are lessons for all of us no matter the state of our own local congregation.

Revelation 3 - 7 Churches Cont.

As we study the last of seven churches in Revelation 3, let's notice how much they look like some modern churches.

Sardis

Revelation 3:1 And unto the angel of the church in Sardis write; These things saith he that hath the seven Spirits of God, and the seven stars; I know thy works, that thou hast a name that thou livest, and art dead.

This church is not indicted for corruption, nor harassed by persecution. It was far worse. It was dead or almost dead, as are many modern western churches. As faith without works is dead (James 2:20, 26), so are works without faith. It's no use *"Having a form of godliness, but denying the power thereof: from such turn away." (2 Timothy 3:5)*

This may also apply to any having a one-way conversation with God, ignoring God's Word, or treating the Bible like a menu, not acknowledging that *"All Scripture is God-breathed" (2 Timothy 3:16 NIV),* or that *"no prophecy was ever made by an act of human will, but men moved by the Holy Spirit spoke from God." (2 Peter 1:21 NASB).*

Spiritual death may also be a danger among those whose focus is physical buildings and man-made traditions, but do not worship *"in spirit and in truth" (John 4:24).*

Revelation 3:2 Be watchful, and strengthen the things which remain, that are ready to die: for I have not found thy works perfect before God.

Even here, in a church about to die, there is hope. Otherwise, there would be no hope in thousands of dead and dying churches across the western world.

Revelation 3:3 Remember therefore how thou hast received and heard, and hold fast, and repent. If therefore thou shalt not watch, I will come on thee as a thief, and thou shalt not know what hour I will come upon thee.

In a dying church, it is tempting to abandon the faith of our ancestors and try a new thing, but Jesus' counsel is the exact opposite, to remember the faith once for all delivered to the saints and hold fast. Surprisingly, many young people are looking for the faith of the apostles, and churches that have returned to it are growing.

Jesus is not a thief, but like a burglar in one way: He will come when we do not expect Him. So much for all our charts and diagrams detailing theoretical events before His return. They may all prove to be a waste of time.

Revelation 3:4 Thou hast a few names even in Sardis which have not defiled their garments; and they shall walk with me in white: for they are worthy.

Even in the most lifeless church in all Christendom, there are a few names. If we look long enough, we will find them. It may be a quiet widow who prays ceaselessly, an elderly veteran who reads his Bible faithfully, a young man quietly meditating on the Proverbs, or a tired mother faithfully teaching her children about God. Such gems are often found in a local church that is otherwise dead and dying.

Revelation 3:5 He that overcometh, the same shall be clothed in white raiment; and I will not blot out his name out of the book of life, but I will confess his name before my Father, and before his angels.

Overcoming in a dying church can be discouraging, but a few nonconformists are very much alive and will wear white in resurrection. Would we feel quite alone in such a church? But, we are not alone. There are thousands of faithful saints on earth and in heaven who join us, cheering us on. Remember Stephen the martyr. He probably felt so alone too, yet upon His death, Jesus was so taken that He stood in respect (Acts 7:56). All heaven is with us! Who can be against us!

Revelation 3:6 He that hath an ear, let him hear what the Spirit saith unto the churches.

Again, let all Christendom heed. Even in a dead church, salvation can be found among those who hear what the Spirit says.

Philadelphia

Revelation 3:7 And to the angel of the church in Philadelphia write; These things saith he that is holy, he that is true, he that hath the key of David, he that openeth, and no man shutteth; and shutteth, and no man openeth;

There are various keys which the Bible refers to: keys to the kingdom which the apostles possessed (Matthew 16:19; 18:18); the key of knowledge (Luke 11:52); the key of death and Hades (Revelation 1:18); the key to the house of God (1 Chronicles 9:27); the key of David (Isaiah 22:22; Revelation 3:7) and the key to the abyss (Revelation 20:1). In some way all these descriptions are relevant. Christ alone opens where no man can shut, and shuts where no man can open.

Revelation 3:8 I know thy works: behold, I have set before thee an open door, and no man can shut it: for thou hast a little strength, and hast kept my word, and hast not denied my name.

This church has an open door, access or entrance into the joy of the Lord, and though little in strength, its members confess the name of Christ.

Revelation 3:9 Behold, I will make them of the synagogue of Satan, which say they are Jews, and are not, but do lie; behold, I will make them to come and worship before thy feet, and to know that I have loved thee.

They are Persecuted by Jews whom Jesus calls not true Jews, who would do the works of Abraham (John 8:39), and is a Jew inwardly (Romans 2:28). These persecuting Jews will be forced to acknowledge that Jesus loved the Christians.

Revelation 3:10 Because thou hast kept the word of my patience, I also will keep thee from the hour of temptation, which shall come upon all the world, to try them that dwell upon the earth.

Keeping these Christians from the hour of trial does not necessarily mean to be taken out of the world in a "secret" rapture, because Jesus prayed that the faithful would be kept from the evil one, the same Greek words (John 17:15). In the apocalyptic genre this "time of trial" can be seen as a general description of many Christian experiences, rather than a specific time yet future, though it can be both.

Revelation 3:11 Behold, I come quickly: hold that fast which thou hast, that no man take thy crown.

The theory of "once saved always saved" is contradicted by verses such as this. The full picture of salvation is that we are saved in a moment, are being saved and will be saved. It's more of a process than a moment in isolation. *"But he who endures to the end shall be saved."* (Matthew 24:13)

Revelation 3:12 Him that overcometh will I make a pillar in the temple of my God, and he shall go no more out: and I will write upon him the name of my God, and the name of the city of my God, which is new Jerusalem, which cometh down out of heaven from my God: and I will write upon him my new name.

The rewards to the churches are interesting. While salvation itself is a free gift (John 3:16; Romans 6:23; Ephesians 2:8), we are rewarded in salvation according to our works (Romans 2:6; 1 Corinthians 3:8; Revelation 22:12). Some will be rewarded with leadership over ten cities (Luke 19:17), some will be rewarded with national and international leadership responsibilities (Revelation 2:26), and Philadelphian overcomers will have great roles within the temple of God.

Because they did not deny God's name (vs 8), they will have new names like one writes important names on a temple pillar, perhaps signifying adoption by God, and of citizenship in New Jerusalem, and God's name as a seal of consecration like the high priests wore (Exodus 28:36-38).

Revelation 3:13 He that hath an ear, let him hear what the Spirit saith unto the churches.

Again, what the Spirit says to Philadelphia we are all to hear.

Laodicea

Revelation 3:14 And unto the angel of the church of the Laodiceans write; These things saith the Amen, the faithful and true witness, the beginning of the creation of God;

Jesus is not a created being, but the Origin or Source of the creation of God. This is perhaps the last and worst of the seven churches. Only this church and Sardis lack any approval from Jesus. It's all bad news, except for the opportunity to be an overcomer, even here.

Revelation 3:15 I know thy works, that thou art neither cold nor hot: I would thou wert cold or hot.

Laodicea was a very wealthy city with horrible water. Much like their water, which came from hot springs via aqueduct, arriving in town luke warm and tasting awful, this church is neither cold like a refreshing glass of water, nor hot like a cup of soup. They are apathetic Christians.

Revelation 3:16 So then because thou art lukewarm, and neither cold nor hot, I will spue thee out of my mouth.

Like their awful town water, Jesus is about to spit them out of His mouth.

Revelation 3:17 Because thou sayest, I am rich, and increased with goods, and have need of nothing; and knowest not that thou art wretched, and miserable, and poor, and blind, and naked:

Unlike poor Smyrna who God counted as rich, Laodicea is the opposite, materially rich yet spiritually poor. Much like Christianity in wealthy countries of Europe, North America, Australia and New Zealand, these folks are in reality *"wretched, and miserable, and poor, and blind, and naked."* In this superlative description, Revelation also uncovers the deception of material wealth.

Revelation 3:18 I counsel thee to buy of me gold tried in the fire, that thou mayest be rich; and white raiment, that thou mayest be clothed, and that the shame of thy nakedness do not appear; and anoint thine eyes with eyesalve, that thou mayest see.

Luxury does not build character, but trials by fire do. This is the true wealth of spiritual standing before God. Though well-dressed by this world's standards, they were spiritually shamefully naked, and counselled to be clothed with the pure white garments of righteousness.

Their world-renowned eye salve did not give them spiritual vision. Like bribes from the devil, wealth can blind us (Deuteronomy 16:19). It can blind even spiritual leaders who must watch over God's flock (Isaiah 56:10), making them blind leaders of the blind

(Matthew 15:14), blind guides (Matthew 23:16).

Revelation 3:19 As many as I love, I rebuke and chasten: be zealous therefore, and repent.

God chastises and disciplines those He loves (Proverbs 3:12; Hebrews 12:6).

Revelation 3:20 Behold, I stand at the door, and knock: if any man hear my voice, and open the door, I will come in to him, and will sup with him, and he with me.

In a possible historical sense, Jesus says to Philadelphia, *"Behold, I come quickly" (verse 11)* and then to Laodicea He is closer to coming, even knocking at the door. In a figurative sense, Jesus is an outsider to this church, desiring to come in. Some few do invite Him in and He has true communion with them.

Revelation 3:21 To him that overcometh will I grant to sit with me in my throne, even as I also overcame, and am set down with my Father in his throne.

To overcome the deception of wealth must indeed be exceptional. This is a remarkable reward, to sit at the very throne of Christ. Whereas some will rule over cities, or nations, and some will have high positions in the temple, these overcomers will be at the throne, perhaps as a part of Christ's inner cabinet.

Revelation 3:22 He that hath an ear, let him hear what the Spirit saith unto the churches.

Whether this is in part an historical sequence or not, it is also at the same time applicable in all times and cultures.

There is no mention of leaving a bad church, nor being self-righteous about ours. The seven churches are what they are, and even in the worst of them, salvation and overcoming are possible.

Revelation 4 - Heavenly Vision

Let's take a look at John's vision of heaven in Revelation 4.

Heaven

Revelation 4:1 After this I looked, and, behold, a door was opened in heaven: and the first voice which I heard was as it were of a trumpet talking with me; which said, Come up hither, and I will shew thee things which must be hereafter.

This seems to refer to the former voice from Revelation 1:10, the voice of Christ, reverberating like a sacred temple trumpet. Since the advent of amplification, we might describe the voice differently today.

Revelation 4:2 And immediately I was in the spirit: and, behold, a throne was set in heaven, and one sat on the throne.

Like a vision, John was transported "in the spirit" through the door into heaven, perhaps in a trance or ecstasy of some kind.

Revelation 4:3 And he that sat was to look upon like a jasper and a sardine stone: and there was a rainbow round about the throne, in sight like unto an emerald.

We have a picture of Jasper of unknown color, perhaps clear white chalcedony [pronounced: kal-SAID-o-knee], along with red Sardius and an emerald green rainbow or glow.

Revelation 4:4 And round about the throne were four and twenty seats: and upon the seats I saw four and twenty elders sitting, clothed in white raiment; and they had on their heads crowns of gold.

Could this picture represent the complete church of God, in both testaments, in the twelve patriarchs of the twelve tribes and the twelve apostles? Is this also pictured in the 24 courses of priests serving in the temple (1 Chronicles 24:1-19)?

Revelation 4:5 And out of the throne proceeded lightnings and thunderings and voices: and there were seven lamps of fire burning before the throne, which are the seven Spirits of God.

Most commentators seem to identify the seven lamps and seven Spirits with seven different manifestations of the Holy Spirit among the seven churches.

Revelation 4:6 And before the throne there was a sea of glass like unto crystal: and in the midst of the throne, and round about the throne, were four beasts [creatures] full of eyes before and behind.

Few like the translation "beasts" as it seems to degrade these angels. A better translation is "living things" or "living creatures." Like the sword out of Jesus' mouth, picturing the sword of the Word of God, we must see these as possibly more symbolic than literal.

Revelation 4:7 And the first beast was like a lion, and the second beast like a calf, and the third beast had a face as a man, and the fourth beast was like a flying eagle.

This reminds us of the symbols associated with at least 3 and perhaps all 4 leading tribes camped about the worship tent in the wilderness. Judah (the lion) was camped on the East with Issachar and Zebulun. Ephraim (the ox) was camped on the West with Manasseh and Benjamin. Reuben (the man) was camped on the South with Gad and Simeon. Dan (the snake) was camped on the North with Asher and Naphtali (the eagle here is unconfirmed, except as a possible symbol of a judge).

Revelation 4:8 And the four beasts had each of them six wings about him; and they were full of eyes within: and they rest not day and night, saying, Holy, holy, holy, Lord God Almighty, which was, and is, and is to come.

These spirit beings are similar to the Seraphs of Isaiah 6:2-3, who also cried "holy, holy, holy." In a symbolic genre, their example of worship is more important than speculation about what the eyes or wings mean. Saying "holy, holy, holy" reminds us of the Trinity and the One who was, and is, and is to come. How often throughout the day do we pause to give a word of thanks or praise to God?

Revelation 4:9 And when those beasts give glory and honour and thanks to him that sat on the throne, who liveth for ever and ever,

Giving glory and honor and thanks is a beautiful summary of what our prayers ought to be.

Revelation 4:10 The four and twenty elders fall down before him that sat on the throne, and worship him that liveth for ever and ever, and cast their crowns before the throne, saying,

Casting crowns is an ancient symbol of surrender and subjection to a conquering king.

Revelation 4:11 Thou art worthy, O Lord [and God], to receive glory and honour and power:

for thou hast created all things, and for thy pleasure they are and were created.

The original language says "Lord and God." When we say that the Lord is worthy, we are saying that we are not worthy. The little word "for" here introduces the reason for "the glory and the honour and the power." None of us created all things. Humanity has no reason for self-glorification, self-honoring or even taking power to self.

The words "for your pleasure" sound like God is self-indulgent in modern English, and are better translated today as "by your will" (NIV, ESV), or "because of Your will they existed, and were created" (NASB). Saying that God is worthy is a simple acknowledgment that we only exist because of His will.

The more we understand the difference between the Good Shepherd, pictured in the Lamb, and the beasts which picture human governments, the more we will love the kingdom of God, and the less appealing the politics of this world will be. John's vision of everyone in heaven and on earth praising our Lord is appropriate. He is worthy, and nobody else is.

Revelation 5 - The Scroll and the Myriad

Let's look at John's vision of the scroll with seven seals and of every creature in heaven and earth worshipping God.

The Scroll

Revelation 5:1 And I saw in the right hand of him that sat on the throne a book written within and on the backside, sealed with seven seals.

A scroll written on both sides indicates the fullness of it. It is similar to the scroll that Ezekiel saw (Ezekiel 2:9-10) filled with lamentation, mourning and woe. The contents of this mysterious scroll are not given. Later we see that its seven seals are divine punishment.

Revelation 5:2 And I saw a strong angel proclaiming with a loud voice, Who is worthy to open the book, and to loose the seals thereof?

Who can reveal the secrets within the scroll?

Revelation 5:3 And no man in heaven, nor in earth, neither under the earth, was able to open the book, neither to look thereon.

Many theories abound, but no man is worthy to reveal the secrets. All we understand about the book is the contents of its seals beginning in Revelation 6, not what is written in the book itself.

Revelation 5:4 And I wept much, because no man was found worthy to open and to read the book, neither to look thereon.

Are we so desirous to understand God's word?

Revelation 5:5 And one of the elders saith unto me, Weep not: behold, the Lion of the tribe of Judah, the Root of David, hath prevailed to open the book, and to loose the seven seals thereof.

Only Jesus can reveal the secrets. Let's see what He has to say.

Revelation 5:6 And I beheld, and, lo, in the midst of the throne and of the four beasts, and in the midst of the elders, stood a Lamb as it had been slain, having seven horns and seven eyes, which are the seven Spirits of God sent forth into all the earth.

This pictures Jesus as an innocent little sacrificial Passover Lamb, living yet slain, a symbol of a different kind of leadership to that of beast-like worldly human governments. The horns of a more mature ram on a little lamb, symbolize God's omnipotence (Deuteronomy 33:17; 1 Kings 22:11; Jeremiah 48:25; Zechariah 1:18; Daniel 7:24; 8:20) and seven symbolizes perfection. The eyes symbolize God's omniscience, as they run to and fro throughout the whole earth (2 Chronicles 16:9). The seven Spirits express perhaps the fullness of the Holy Spirit or the seven angels in the seven churches, apostled or sent forth into all the earth (Zechariah 3:9; 4:10).

Revelation 5:7 And he came and took the book out of the right hand of him that sat upon the throne.

Jesus takes the book from God the Father.

Revelation 5:8 And when he had taken the book, the four beasts and four and twenty elders fell down before the Lamb, having every one of them harps, and golden vials full of odours, which are the prayers of saints.

Our prayers are symbolized as incense, a pleasant odor in heaven.

Revelation 5:9 And they sung a new song, saying, Thou art worthy to take the book, and to open the seals thereof: for thou wast slain, and hast redeemed us to God by thy blood out of every kindred, and tongue, and people, and nation;

Our songs on earth are often imperfect, so we need a new song, not with doubtful human words but pure. This will be sung by resurrected saints from everywhere.

Revelation 5:10 And hast made us unto our God kings and priests: and we shall reign on the earth.

Remember: "*But you are a chosen generation, a royal priesthood, a holy nation, His own special people, that you may proclaim the praises of Him who called you out of darkness into His marvelous light*" (1 Peter 2:9)

The Myriad

Revelation 5:11 And I beheld, and I heard the voice of many angels round about the throne and the beasts and the elders: and the number of them was ten thousand times ten thousand, and thousands of thousands;

Myriad, in some translations, literally means ten thousand and figuratively a very large number.

Revelation 5:12 Saying with a loud voice, Worthy is the Lamb that was slain to receive power, and riches, and wisdom, and strength, and honour, and glory, and blessing.

Who else is worthy? None of us.

Revelation 5:13 And every creature which is in heaven, and on the earth, and under the earth, and such as are in the sea, and all that are in them, heard I saying, Blessing, and honour, and glory, and power, be unto him that sitteth upon the throne, and unto the Lamb for ever and ever.

How is this possible to see except as an awesome vision?

Revelation 5:14 And the four beasts said, Amen. And the four and twenty elders fell down and worshipped him that liveth for ever and ever.

This song of the redeemed is not just sung but includes ceremonial acts in several parts: the four creatures, the 24 elders, and the myriad each in turn carry out their symbolic acts.

The more we understand the difference between the Good Shepherd, pictured in the Lamb, and the beasts which picture human governments, the more we will love the kingdom of God, and the less appealing the politics of this world will be. John's vision of everyone in heaven and on earth praising our Lord is appropriate. He is worthy, and nobody else is.

Revelation 6 - 4 Horsemen

Let's see what happens as Jesus opens the first six seals of the mysterious scroll.

1st Seal - White Horse

Revelation 6:1-2 And I saw when the Lamb opened one of the seals, and I heard, as it were the noise of thunder, one of the four beasts saying, Come and see. And I saw, and behold a white horse: and he that sat on him had a bow; and a crown was given unto him: and he went forth conquering, and to conquer.

The white horse is commonly seen as the conquest of Roman imperialism, various antichrist figures, or warfare in general. Some include Christ and the Gospel in that warfare as He conquers evil and through Him, the church is triumphant, overcoming spiritual battles.

2nd Seal - Red Horse

Revelation 6:3-4 And when he had opened the second seal, I heard the second beast say, Come and see. And there went out another horse that was red: and power was given to him that sat thereon to take peace from the earth, and that they should kill one another: and there was given unto him a great sword.

The red horse seems to symbolize variously the bloodshed caused by the Roman system, and all similar systems of human oppression throughout history, and the persecution of Christians.

3rd Seal - Black Horse

Revelation 6:5-6 And when he had opened the third seal, I heard the third beast say, Come and see. And I beheld, and lo a black horse; and he that sat on him had a pair of balances in his hand. And I heard a voice in the midst of the four beasts say, A measure of wheat for a penny, and three measures of barley for a penny; and see thou hurt not the oil and the wine.

The black horse seems to symbolize variously the deprivation caused by the failure of all human economic systems and the famines caused by warfare.

4th Seal - Pale Horse

Revelation 6:7-8 And when he had opened the fourth seal, I heard the voice of the fourth beast say, Come and see. And I looked, and behold a pale horse: and his name that sat on him was Death, and Hell followed with him. And power was given unto them over the fourth part of the earth, to kill with sword, and with hunger, and with death, and with the beasts of the earth.

The pale horse clearly symbolizes death and Hades, and a large percentage of people dying by various means. These first four seals symbolize the woes that accompany believers living in this world.

5th Seal - Martyrs

Revelation 6:9-11 And when he had opened the fifth seal, I saw under the altar the souls of them that were slain for the word of God, and for the testimony which they held: And they cried with a loud voice, saying, How long, O Lord, holy and true, dost thou not judge and avenge our blood on them that dwell on the earth? And white robes were given unto every one of them; and it was said unto them, that they should rest yet for a little season, until their fellowservants also and their brethren, that should be killed as they were, should be fulfilled.

These are the martyrs of the Christian faith past, present and future, pictured as under the altar, where the blood of sacrifices was spilled.

6th Seal - Cosmic Signs

Revelation 6:12-14 And I beheld when he had opened the sixth seal, and, lo, there was a great earthquake; and the sun became black as sackcloth of hair, and the moon became as blood; And the stars of heaven fell unto the earth, even as a fig tree casteth her untimely figs, when she is shaken of a mighty wind. And the heaven departed as a scroll when it is rolled together; and every mountain and island were moved out of their places.

A preterist view of this is a societal earthquake and the shake up of political leaders pictured by sun, moon and stars in the fall of Jerusalem. An historical view might include the fall of pagan Rome to Christianity, and a futurist view might see these catastrophic signs right before the Second Coming. The symbolic or spiritual view can see all these as valid facets of the struggle between good and evil.

Revelation 6:15-17 And the kings of the earth, and the great men, and the rich men, and the chief captains, and the mighty men, and every bondman, and every free man, hid themselves in the dens and in the rocks of the mountains; And said to the mountains and rocks, Fall on us, and hide us from the face of him that sitteth on the throne, and from the wrath of the Lamb: For the great day of his wrath is come; and who shall be able to stand?

This clearly moves the emphasis from any forerunners or prototypes, such as a preterist view of the fall of Jerusalem, or an historical view of the conquest of Rome by Christianity in Constantine's time, to its final fulfillment at the Second Coming. These ideas pale into insignificance compared to their final fulfillment at Christ's return.

Revelation 7 - The Sealed

Let's take a look at the sealing of the faithful among all nations, beginning with Israel in Revelation 7.

Israel Sealed

Revelation 7:1 And after these things I saw four angels standing on the four corners [angles] of the earth, holding the four winds of the earth, that the wind should not blow on the earth, nor on the sea, nor on any tree.

The four corners, angles or compass points of the land are still used today. Winds are pictured as scattering the ancient nation of Elam (Jeremiah 49:36-37), as an attack by the enemy nation of Babylon (Jeremiah 51:1-2) and a spiritual battle with false doctrine (Ephesians 4:14).

Revelation 7:2-3 And I saw another angel ascending from the east, having the seal of the living God: and he cried with a loud voice to the four angels, to whom it was given to hurt the earth and the sea, Saying, Hurt not the earth, neither the sea, nor the trees, till we have sealed the servants of our God in their foreheads.

People must eventually decide to either have the mark of the beast, a trust in worldly politics and human solutions, sealed in their foreheads or the seal of God, the Holy Spirit. The people of God are certainly sealed by the Holy Spirit (2 Corinthians 1:22) as a seal of belonging (2 Timothy 2:19) and a seal of holiness (Exodus 39:30).

Revelation 7:4 And I heard the number of them which were sealed: and there were sealed an hundred and forty and four thousand of all the tribes of the children of Israel.

Are these literally physical Israel now converted to the true faith? Once first among the nations, they became among the last because they rejected Christ, now are they counted first once again after the conversion of many Jews just before Christ's return?

Revelation 7:5 Of the tribe of Juda were sealed twelve thousand. Of the tribe of Reuben were sealed twelve thousand. Of the tribe of Gad were sealed twelve thousand.

No longer is Reuben counted first, the literal firstborn, yet unstable as water (Genesis 49:3-4), has been replaced. Judah, the tribe from which our Lord sprang, has taken first place among the twelve.

Revelation 7:6 Of the tribe of Aser were sealed twelve thousand. Of the tribe of Nephthalim were sealed twelve thousand. Of the tribe of Manasses were sealed twelve thousand.

Manasseh was one of the sons of Joseph, here counted separately and Dan is now missing, possibly because they left their inherited land and began worshipping pagan gods. They eventually disappeared as a people from history. This possibly also symbolizes Judas Iscariot who betrayed his place among the Apostles and so a substitute, Matthaias was chosen (Acts 1:15-26).

Revelation 7:7-8 Of the tribe of Simeon were sealed twelve thousand. Of the tribe of Levi were sealed twelve thousand. Of the tribe of Issachar were sealed twelve thousand. Of the tribe of Zabulon were sealed twelve thousand. Of the tribe of Joseph were sealed twelve thousand. Of the tribe of Benjamin were sealed twelve thousand.

The inheritance of Joseph now falls upon his second son Ephraim, who received the birthright of the first son. Thus bringing the number of the tribes back up to twelve, in a similar manner that a substitute was required for the twelve Apostles.

All Nations Sealed

Revelation 7:9 After this I beheld, and, lo, a great multitude, which no man could number, of all nations, and kindreds, and people, and tongues, stood before the throne, and before the Lamb, clothed with white robes, and palms in their hands;

Are the 144,000 literal Israel or spiritual Israel? We are not told. If spiritual Israel is intended, the church, then who are these other people also dressed in white, a symbol of righteousness? These other nations are also therefore in the church.

Let's not wildly speculate, but be satisfied with the words as they are, and with the mystery of what is not said, for now. The use of palms elsewhere symbolizes rejoicing in the Lord at the Feast of Tabernacles (Leviticus 23:40) and Jesus' victory parade (John 12:13).

Revelation 7:10 And cried with a loud voice, saying, Salvation to our God which sitteth upon the throne, and unto the Lamb.

These are also the saved, giving praise to the source of their salvation. So, the theory that only the symbolic 144,000 are saved is wrong.

Revelation 7:11-12 And all the angels stood round about the throne, and about the elders and the four beasts, and fell before the throne on their faces, and worshipped God, Saying, Amen: Blessing, and glory, and wisdom, and thanksgiving, and honour, and power, and might, be unto our God for ever and ever. Amen.

This 7-fold doxology is an anthem of complete praise.

Revelation 7:13-14 And one of the elders answered, saying unto me, What are these which are arrayed in white robes? and whence came they? And I said unto him, Sir, thou knowest. And he said to me, These are they which came out of [the] great tribulation, and have washed their robes, and made them white in the blood of the Lamb.

The Great Tribulation is that which was foretold by our Lord and Daniel (Matthew 24:21; Daniel 12:1) and results in persecution and suffering and martyrdom of the people who are washed in the blood of the Lamb.

Revelation 7:15-17 Therefore are they before the throne of God, and serve him day and night in his temple: and he that sitteth on the throne shall dwell among them. They shall hunger no more, neither thirst any more; neither shall the sun light on them, nor any heat. For the Lamb which is in the midst of the throne shall feed them, and shall lead them unto living fountains of waters: and God shall wipe away all tears from their eyes.

Using words from Isaiah 49:10, this is a time when the plight of an oppressed people is over. There is no more hunger or thirst of starved and persecuted Christians, no more heat of fiery trials, no more tears, just the Lamb, a feast and life-giving water.

When the faithful of Israel and the nations are sealed, will we be among them?

Revelation 8 - 7th Seal 1st 4 Trumpets

Let's look at the punishment of those who persecuted the church, the final of seven seals and the first four of seven trumpets.

7th Seal - Silence

Revelation 8:1 And when he had opened the seventh seal, there was silence in heaven about the space of half an hour.

Whether or not the seals or the scroll is being revealed is unclear, so we will leave it at that and be satisfied with the mystery. Sometimes silence in the church is a good thing. This silence seems to be profound and expectant.

Revelation 8:2 And I saw the seven angels which stood before God; and to them were given seven trumpets.

Trumpets were blown at sacred assemblies, as a signal to move camp and as an alarm of war (Numbers 10:4-9). A whole festival was set aside specifically as a memorial of blowing of trumpets (Leviticus 23:23-25).

Revelation 8:3-4 And another angel came and stood at the altar, having a golden censer; and there was given unto him much incense, that he should offer it with the prayers of all saints upon the golden altar which was before the throne. And the smoke of the incense, which came with the prayers of the saints, ascended up before God out of the angel's hand.

A golden vessel mixes the prayers of the saints with incense. The golden censer was part of the Temple furniture behind the veil, within the Holy of Holies (1 Kings 7:50; 2 Chronicles 4:22; Hebrews 9:1-5). It was only accessed on the Day of Atonement and so this is a very special vessel for a very special occasion. How precious must God regard the prayers of His saints sanctified by Christ's Atonement (Psalm 141:1-2; Ephesians 5:1-2)!

Revelation 8:5 And the angel took the censer, and filled it with fire of the altar, and cast it into the earth: and there were voices, and thunderings, and lightnings, and an earthquake.

God's answer to the prayers of His suffering saints is fire on earth, good news for the church, but bad news for the church's foes.

Revelation 8:6 And the seven angels which had the seven trumpets prepared themselves to sound.

1st Trumpet - Fire & Blood

Revelation 8:7 The first angel sounded, and there followed hail and fire mingled with blood, and they were cast upon the earth: and the third part of trees was burnt up, and all green grass was burnt up.

Is this literal ecological disaster of great magnitude or are the trees and grass symbolic of people destroyed who persecuted the church as a final warning for them to repent? A parallel with the plagues of the Exodus is unmistakable.

2nd Trumpet - Fire Mountain

Revelation 8:8-9 And the second angel sounded, and as it were a great mountain burning with fire was cast into the sea: and the third part of the sea became blood; And the third part of the creatures which were in the sea, and had life, died; and the third part of the ships were destroyed.

A mountain symbolizes a human government. Israel was God's holy mountain (Exodus 15:17) and Babylon was a destroying mountain (Jeremiah 51:25, 42). A mountain burning with fire can signify a volcanic event. Certainly an allusion to the Egyptian plagues is evident, punishing those who persecuted the church.

3rd Trumpet - Fallen Star

Revelation 8:10-11 And the third angel sounded, and there fell a great star from heaven, burning as it were a lamp, and it fell upon the third part of the rivers, and upon the fountains of waters; And the name of the star is called Wormwood: and the third part of the waters became wormwood; and many men died of the waters, because they were made bitter.

This is interpreted by many wildly speculative means, but an old prophecy gives some meaning. As Jerusalem rejected the fountain of living waters, and hewed broken cisterns that could not hold water, so many have chased after modern versions of idolatry (Jeremiah 2:1-13).

4th Trumpet - Sun, Moon & Stars

Revelation 8:12-13 And the fourth angel sounded, and the third part of the sun was smitten, and the third part of the moon, and the third part of the stars; so as the third part of them was darkened, and the day shone not for a third part of it, and the night likewise. And I beheld, and heard an angel flying through the midst of heaven, saying with a loud voice, Woe, woe, woe, to the inhabiters of the earth by reason of the other voices of the trumpet of the three angels, which are yet to sound!

With imagery long used in ancient prophecies depicting the fall of nations and national leaders, this can apply to the fall of Jerusalem, the fall of Rome and even the fall of a yet future Beast power. Woe, woe, woe seems to imply a worsening of world events just before Christ's Second Coming.

Let's never forget that what we are reading pictures the victory of the church over evil in the world.

Revelation 9 - First 2 Woes

Let's now take a look at the fifth and sixth trumpets, also known as the first two of three woes, in Revelation 9.

5th Trumpet 1st Woe - The Abyss

Revelation 9:1 And the fifth angel sounded, and I saw a star fall from heaven unto the earth: and to him was given the key of the bottomless pit.

A star falling from heaven to earth is reminiscent of Lucifer (Isaiah 14:12-14; Ezekiel 28:14-18; Luke 10:18) and the bottomless pit, better rendered as the abyss, elsewhere mentioned as a place of restraint for the demons (Luke 8:31; 2 Peter 2:4).

Revelation 9:2 And he opened the bottomless pit; and there arose a smoke out of the pit, as the smoke of a great furnace; and the sun and the air were darkened by reason of the smoke of the pit.

Are demons let loose for a while? The influence of such evil ones is the opposite of the smoke of the incense or our prayers. It is a smoke that blocks out the light of the glorious gospel.

Revelation 9:3 And there came out of the smoke locusts upon the earth: and unto them was given power, as the scorpions of the earth have power.

Locusts are suggestive of a swarm, but unlike ordinary locusts, these arise from the smoke coming out of the pit with deadly power, like that of a large army (Joel 2).

Revelation 9:4 And it was commanded them that they should not hurt the grass of the earth, neither any green thing, neither any tree; but only those men which have not the seal of God in their foreheads.

These armies of locusts will only hurt the non-Christians, those not sealed by the Holy Spirit in their foreheads, but having the mark of the beast instead.

Revelation 9:5 And to them it was given that they should not kill them, but that they should be tormented five months: and their torment was as the torment of a scorpion, when he striketh a man.

The natural time of a locust plague can be 5 months, often from April to September. This can also mean 150 prophetic days or years, or it can also be symbolic of a short time.

Revelation 9:6 And in those days shall men seek death, and shall not find it; and shall desire to die, and death shall flee from them.

This seeking death is descriptive of extraordinary suffering, whereby death would bring relief.

Revelation 9:7 And the shapes of the locusts were like unto horses prepared unto battle; and on their heads were as it were crowns like gold, and their faces were as the faces of men.

Locusts look like they have little like horseheads and are called little horses in several languages. It's easy to imagine a war machine and battle helmets in this imagery.

Revelation 9:8 And they had hair as the hair of women, and their teeth were as the teeth of lions.

Perhaps these are warriors from a culture where men grow long hair like women. Perhaps something about their helmet or equipment gives them this appearance.

Revelation 9:9 And they had breastplates, as it were breastplates of iron; and the sound of their wings was as the sound of chariots of many horses running to battle.

This is reminiscent of the sound of a great army. Modern war machines, such as attack helicopters are also very loud. The spiritual battle in the world also rages on.

Revelation 9:10 And they had tails like unto scorpions, and there were stings in their tails: and their power was to hurt men five months.

Again the damage done by these is limited in time.

Revelation 9:11 And they had a king over them, which is the angel of the bottomless pit, whose name in the Hebrew tongue is Abaddon, but in the Greek tongue hath his name Apollyon.

The angel of the abyss is probably the devil. The name Abaddon or Apollyon signifies the destroyer and the son of destruction (2 Thessalonians 2:3-4).

Revelation 9:12 One woe is past; and, behold, there come two woes more hereafter.

So, each of these last 3 trumpets is a woe.

6th Trumpet 2nd Woe - 200 Million

Revelation 9:13 And the sixth angel sounded, and I heard a voice from the four horns of the golden altar which is before God,

Picturing heaven in such language ties the Old Testament Temple, with its golden altar of incense, and the New Testament together as one unified revelation of God.

Revelation 9:14 Saying to the sixth angel which had the trumpet, Loose the four angels which are bound in the great river Euphrates.

Important events are often initiated by angels. These angels are bound, and thus likely demons, symbolically captive in Babylon.

Revelation 9:15 And the four angels were loosed, which were prepared for an hour, and a day, and a month, and a year, for to slay the third part of men.

This is literally "the" hour, and day, and month, and year. These angels were prepared for a specific time in God's Divine plan.

Revelation 9:16 And the number of the army of the horsemen were two hundred thousand thousand: and I heard the number of them.

A two hundred million man army is myriads of myriads, which if literal, only a large Asian population east of the Euphrates could muster. Then again, this prophecy is in apocalyptic or symbolic language and could portray a demonic army or all armies throughout human history.

Revelation 9:17 And thus I saw the horses in the vision, and them that sat on them, having breastplates of fire, and of jacinth, and brimstone: and the heads of the horses were as the heads of lions; and out of their mouths issued fire and smoke and brimstone.

There is a possibility that John is describing modern weapons.

Revelation 9:18 By these three was the third part of men killed, by the fire, and by the smoke, and by the brimstone, which issued out of their mouths.

This is a large death toll indeed.

Revelation 9:19 For their power is in their mouth, and in their tails: for their tails were like unto serpents, and had heads, and with them they do hurt.

There is power in weapons and in false doctrines to hurt.

Revelation 9:20 And the rest of the men which were not killed by these plagues yet repented not of the works of their hands, that they should not worship devils, and idols of gold, and silver, and brass, and stone, and of wood: which neither can see, nor hear, nor walk:

The purpose of these plagues is to bring men to repentance, but to no avail, as they continue to worship things made by human hands. These are men who will not believe in God without such evidence as supernatural plagues.

Revelation 9:21 Neither repented they of their murders, nor of their sorceries, nor of their fornication, nor of their thefts.

This exposes the lie of atheism, falsely claiming that there is no evidence for God. Atheists seem to have gotten away with suppressing the obvious truth, those things which are clearly seen, yet they are without excuse, their foolish hearts became darkened and they made excuses for many evils they have committed (Romans 1:18-32).

God gives humanity space to repent. Let's not waste the time.

Revelation 10 - Little Book

Let's take a look at the little book in the hand of an angel described in Revelation 10.

The Little Book

Revelation 10:1 And I saw another mighty angel come down from heaven, clothed with a cloud: and a rainbow was upon his head, and his face was as it were the sun, and his feet as pillars of fire:

The description "mighty angel" seems to indicate one of high rank, powerful enough for the superhuman task given, and different from the seven angels with the seven trumpets.

Revelation 10:2 And he had in his hand a little book open: and he set his right foot upon the sea, and his left foot on the earth,

Theories are that the little book, little scroll or booklet is the Bible, the Book of Revelation, or just chapter 11. Let's not fall into the trap of wild speculation, but be satisfied with not knowing everything. The angel sets foot on sea and land together, perhaps signifying authority over both.

Revelation 10:3 And cried with a loud voice, as when a lion roareth: and when he had cried, seven thunders uttered their voices.

The angel cries with a loud voice commanding attention. Then seven others spoke with voices that sounded like thunder and as with the other symbols, wild speculation abounds, dissatisfied with leaving it as a mystery. One has a sense of powerful angels steadfastly loyal to God and disgusted at the unrepentance of humanity.

Revelation 10:4 And when the seven thunders had uttered their voices, I was about to write: and I heard a voice from heaven saying unto me, Seal up those things which the seven thunders uttered, and write them not.

Whatever the seven thunders uttered is not to be revealed as yet, perhaps so that we don't get lost, as many do, in seeking the revelation of twigs of prophecy instead of remaining focused on the main purpose of the book.

Revelation 10:5-6 And the angel which I saw stand upon the sea and upon the earth lifted up his hand to heaven, And sware by him that liveth for ever and ever, who created heaven, and the things that therein are, and the earth, and the things that therein are, and the sea, and the things which are therein, that there should be time no longer:

Swear here means affirm or promise with an oath. Where did our modern courtroom practice come from? Are those Christians who refuse to make an oath in court aware of these verses? What does it mean "time no longer"? Other translations render this that there will be "no more delay." (NIV, NLT, ESV)

Revelation 10:7 But in the days of the voice of the seventh angel, when he shall begin to sound, the mystery of God should be finished, as he hath declared to his servants the prophets.

That there will be no more delay, no more space to repent, is confirmed by the words "the mystery of God should be finished." God's mystery is the opposite of the mystery of Babylon (Revelation 17:5) and its associated mystery of iniquity (2 Thessalonians 2:7). God's mystery has to do with the resurrection of the dead and the mystery of the gospel (1 Corinthians 15:51-52).

Revelation 10:8-9 And the voice which I heard from heaven spake unto me again, and said, Go and take the little book which is open in the hand of the angel which standeth upon the sea and upon the earth. And I went unto the angel, and said unto him, Give me the little book. And he said unto me, Take it, and eat it up; and it shall make thy belly bitter, but it shall be in thy mouth sweet as honey.

Take and eat a book? This figurative language is similar to the scroll given to Ezekiel (3:1-3). We would describe it even today as digesting the contents of a book.

Revelation 10:10 And I took the little book out of the angel's hand, and ate it up; and it was in my mouth sweet as honey: and as soon as I had eaten it, my belly was bitter.

While the gospel is good news, it is only so in contrast to the bad news all around us. Mature Christians will mourn for the sins of the world.

Revelation 10:11 And he said unto me, Thou must prophesy again before many peoples, and nations, and tongues, and kings.

The job of a prophet is not one of bringing only good news, but also a warning. Even many Christians only want to have smooth things preached to them (Isaiah 30:9-13).

The mystery of God and His salvation is only bad news to those who don't want to repent, but want to continue in their sins. God gives them a little space to repent, but that time is limited.

Revelation 11 - 3rd Woe

Let's now take a look at the two witnesses and the seventh trump, otherwise called the third woe.

The Two Witnesses

Revelation 11:1 And there was given me a reed like unto a rod: and the angel stood, saying, Rise, and measure the temple of God, and the altar, and them that worship therein.

Christians may recall that "you are the temple of God" (1 Corinthians 3:16; 2 Corinthians 6:14-7:1) built upon "the foundation of the apostles and prophets, Jesus Christ Himself being the chief cornerstone" (Ephesians 2:19-22). Measurements of a building under construction would include making sure that it's being built firmly on its foundation.

Revelation 11:2 But the court which is without the temple leave out, and measure it not; for it is given unto the Gentiles: and the holy city shall they tread under foot forty and two months.

The court of the gentiles was outside the physical temple. In this context it represents those from all nations not yet fully in the church of God, and perhaps also those of the world who tread the church under foot, trying to mix worldly ideas into the faith, who in reality sit on the outer edges, not actually measured or not fully included in the church of God. This contradicts any who believe in inclusiveness without boundaries, and any who add vain fads and traditions of the world not measured by the teachings of the apostles, prophets and Christ.

Revelation 11:3 And I will give power unto my two witnesses, and they shall prophesy a thousand two hundred and threescore days, clothed in sackcloth.

Amidst much speculation, nobody really knows who the two witnesses are. However, all agree that forty two months is the 1260 days, and three and a half years (time, times and half a time). As half of seven years, this possibly symbolizes shortened time and parallels similar periods in the OT (Daniel 7:25; 12:7).

Revelation 11:4 These are the two olive trees, and the two candlesticks standing before the God of the earth.

This is referring to Zechariah 4 where a hint is given, referring to the ministries of those responsible for finishing the Temple, which may be a type of the final completion of building the church.

Revelation 11:5 And if any man will hurt them, fire proceedeth out of their mouth, and devoureth their enemies: and if any man will hurt them, he must in this manner be killed.

This may refer to literal fire as Elijah called down fire from heaven (2 Kings 1:10), or the symbolic fire of powerful preaching coming from their mouths, which destroys unrepentant attitudes (Jeremiah 1:9-10), or both.

Revelation 11:6 These have power to shut heaven, that it rain not in the days of their prophecy: and have power over waters to turn them to blood, and to smite the earth with all plagues, as often as they will.

This is "authorized power" from heaven.

Revelation 11:7 And when they shall have finished their testimony, the beast that ascendeth out of the bottomless pit shall make war against them, and shall overcome them, and kill them.

This is a beast-spirit which is in total opposition to the Spirit of Christ. In Daniel, beasts are symbolic of human kings and human governments, first is king Nebucchadnezzar

(Daniel 4:16), and then four successive Empires after him: Babylon, Medo-Persia, Greece and Rome (Daniel 7). The beast-spirit from the pit is the true power behind the scenes of these infamous world governments.

Revelation 11:8 And their dead bodies shall lie in the street of the great city, which spiritually is called Sodom and Egypt, where also our Lord was crucified.

Spiritually, today's Jerusalem is not yet the "city of peace" but Sodom and Egypt, perversion, oppression of the poor and slavery to sin.

Revelation 11:9 And they of the people and kindreds and tongues and nations shall see their dead bodies three days and an half, and shall not suffer their dead bodies to be put in graves.

Are these 3½ days the same as the 3½ years? Possibly. On the other hand, with modern broadcasting, it is possible for the whole world to see their bodies in such a short time.

Revelation 11:10 And they that dwell upon the earth shall rejoice over them, and make merry, and shall send gifts one to another; because these two prophets tormented them that dwelt on the earth.

Only evil, unrepentant people would rejoice over such a death.

Revelation 11:11 And after three days and an half the spirit of life from God entered into them, and they stood upon their feet; and great fear fell upon them which saw them.

This resurrection of the two witnesses echoes the valley of dry bones (Ezekiel 37:1-10).

Revelation 11:12 And they heard a great voice from heaven saying unto them, Come up hither. And they ascended up to heaven in a cloud; and their enemies beheld them.

What a contradiction of all things apostate and in rebellion against God, and what a comfort to all faithful preachers of the Word who suffer opposition!

Revelation 11:13 And the same hour was there a great earthquake, and the tenth part of the city fell, and in the earthquake were slain of men seven thousand: and the remnant were affrighted, and gave glory to the God of heaven.

Why should it take such an event before people repent! This emphasizes the stubbornness of humanity.

Revelation 11:14 The second woe is past; and, behold, the third woe cometh quickly.

With the resurrection of the two witnesses and a great earthquake, we understand that the second woe is finished and we are now introduced to the final woe, which is the seventh trumpet.

The 7th Trump 3rd Woe - Chorus

Revelation 11:15 And the seventh angel sounded; and there were great voices in heaven, saying, The kingdoms of this world are become the kingdoms of our Lord, and of his Christ; and he shall reign for ever and ever.

The Hallelujah Chorus quotes these very words.

Revelation 11:16-17 And the four and twenty elders, which sat before God on their seats, fell upon their faces, and worshipped God, Saying, We give thee thanks, O Lord God Almighty, which art, and wast, and art to come; because thou hast taken to thee thy great power, and hast reigned.

In a supreme act of worship, the church's representatives through all ages, give thanks that the hour has finally come.

Revelation 11:18 And the nations were angry, and thy wrath is come, and the time of the dead, that they should be judged, and that thou shouldest give reward unto thy servants the prophets, and to the saints, and them that fear thy name, small and great; and shouldest destroy them which destroy the earth.

The attitude of the nations is revealed as early as Psalm 2:1 and Psalm 99:1, anger instead of repentance.

Revelation 11:19 And the temple of God was opened in heaven, and there was seen in his temple the ark of his testament: and there were lightnings, and voices, and thunderings, and an earthquake, and great hail.

Archaeological digs search for the ark of the covenant. Is this where it went, or was the ark on earth only symbolic of the one in heaven? We can speculate, but what is clear is that the ark was in the holy of holies, which was opened at the cross, when the veil was torn in two (Matthew 27:51).

Preparation for the return of Christ and the fulness of the kingdom has involved suffering and sacrifice, but when it finally comes, the joy will far outweigh anything we will have suffered in this material existence.

Revelation 12 - The Woman

Let's begin to understand the mystery of the woman who gave birth to a child and was persecuted by the dragon.

The Woman

Revelation 12:1 And there appeared a great wonder in heaven; a woman clothed with the sun, and the moon under her feet, and upon her head a crown of twelve stars:

At first glance, this appears to be speaking of Israel and Mary, but as we shall see by the end of the chapter, it has a deeper meaning, because there are others who are included as children of this woman who is in heaven. This is our mother, New Jerusalem (Revelation 12:2, 9-12). Israel is both a mother who gave birth to Jesus (Micah 4:10; 5:3; Song of Solomon 6:10), and a Bride (Isaiah 54:5; 61:10; 62:5).

Revelation 12:2 And she being with child cried, travailing in birth, and pained to be delivered.

The Jewish church gave birth to the Savior and His Bride the Christian Church.

Revelation 12:3 And there appeared another wonder in heaven; and behold a great red dragon, having seven heads and ten horns, and seven crowns upon his heads.

The dragon is symbolic of the evil one.

Revelation 12:4 And his tail drew the third part of the stars of heaven, and did cast them to the earth: and the dragon stood before the woman which was ready to be delivered, for to devour her child as soon as it was born.

This is commonly understood as describing a third of the angels turning bad and becoming demons.

Revelation 12:5 And she brought forth a man child, who was to rule all nations with a rod of iron: and her child was caught up unto God, and to his throne.

This is obviously Jesus.

Revelation 12:6 And the woman fled into the wilderness, where she hath a place prepared of God, that they should feed her there a thousand two hundred and threescore days.

1260 days equals 42 months and 3 1/2 years.

Revelation 12:7 And there was war in heaven: Michael and his angels fought against the dragon; and the dragon fought and his angels,

The timing of this appears to be around the birth of Christ and seems to refer to the spiritual battle that necessitated Christ's parents fleeing to Egypt for a time. However, it also seems to be looking back at a previous time in distant antiquity when the devil was cast out of heaven (Luke 10:18). It also pictures the spiritual battle faced by the church.

Revelation 12:8-9 And prevailed not; neither was their place found any more in heaven. And the great dragon was cast out, that old serpent, called the Devil, and Satan, which deceiveth the whole world: he was cast out into the earth, and his angels were cast out with him.

This is how they ended up in the abyss or prison (2 Peter 2:4) often translated as hell, but is the only scripture where a word loaned from Greek mythology, *tartaroo* is used, picturing an abyss or dungeon of torment.

Revelation 12:10 And I heard a loud voice saying in heaven, Now is come salvation, and strength, and the kingdom of our God, and the power of his Christ: for the accuser of our brethren is cast down, which accused [accuses] them before our God day and night.

The word "accused" is "accuses" in Greek, revealing an ongoing false accusation from the devil. Michael the archangel did not return accusation for accusation against the devil, but instead said, "The Lord rebuke you." (Jude 9). King David was inspired to write Psalm 109 as a prayer against his accusers.

Revelation 12:11 And they overcame him by the blood of the Lamb, and by the word of their testimony; and they loved not their lives unto the death.

How do we overcome the devil? All accusations, true and false, are covered by faith in the blood of the Lamb. If our testimony is to be true, it must be based on the Word of God (John 17:17). Jesus said, "If you abide in My word, you are My disciples indeed." (John 8:31) The paradox of Christianity is that if we love our lives, we are in danger of losing them (John 12:25). Not every Christian will become a martyr, as many still are in countries where persecution exists, but are we willing to live self-sacrificially (Romans 12:1)?

Revelation 12:12 Therefore rejoice, ye heavens, and ye that dwell in them. Woe to the inhabiters of the earth and of the sea! for the devil is come down unto you, having great wrath, because he knoweth that he hath but a short time.

This is literally "woe to the earth and the sea." This describes the suffering of everything that exists on planet earth and its primary cause, the devil.

Revelation 12:13-14 And when the dragon saw that he was cast unto the earth, he persecuted the woman which brought forth the man child. And to the woman were given two wings of a great eagle, that she might fly into the wilderness, into her place, where she is nourished for a time, and times, and half a time, from the face of the serpent.

Two wings of an eagle are used in the Exodus (Exodus 19:4). David and Elijah fled into the wilderness to escape persecution (1 Samuel 23:14-15; 1 Kings 19:4). Mary and Joseph fled to Egypt (Matthew 2:13–23). Persecutions against the New Testament church have been many and varied, from the earliest persecutions by Jews and Romans, then Persian and Islamic persecutions, then Christian to Christian persecutions, Nazi and Communist persecutions, and contemporary persecution across North Africa and Asia. 1260 days adds up to 42 months and three and a half years, a time, times and half a time.

Revelation 12:15 And the serpent cast out of his mouth water as a flood after the woman, that he might cause her to be carried away of the flood.

The flood can symbolize an invading army (Jeremiah 46:7-8; Jeremiah 47:2; Isaiah 8:7-8), ungodliness (2 Samuel 22:5, Psalm 18:4), and a flood of wickedness and evil things (1 Peter 4:4; Proverbs 15:28).

Revelation 12:16 And the earth helped the woman, and the earth opened her mouth, and swallowed up the flood which the dragon cast out of his mouth.

This occurred where Moses' persecutors Korah, Dathan and Abiram, were swallowed up by the earth (Numbers 16:30-32). The earth is perhaps also symbolic of an earthly power which may be quite corrupt in other ways but helps the church, such as Constantine legalizing the southern European church, various civil rulers protecting the Waldensians in the European Alps, and Frederick the Wise protecting Luther.

Revelation 12:17 And the dragon was wroth with the woman, and went to make war with the remnant of her seed, which keep the commandments of God, and have the testimony of Jesus Christ.

Here we see that others are also children of this woman. They are those who keep God's commandments and have the testimony of Christ, obviously referring to the church, mother Zion (Isaiah 66:5-11) and Jerusalem above (Galatians 4:26).

For Christians, keeping God's commandments is in the spirit and not the letter as Jesus explained in the Sermon on the Mount (Matthew 5-7) and Paul taught (2 Corinthians 3:6) and as Jesus testified, the spiritual keeping of God's commandments is summarized by the word love (Matthew 22:36-40). The testimony of Jesus is central to Christianity, trumping the twin heresies of traditionalist legalism and modernist liberalism.

Revelation 13 - The Two Beasts

Do you remember the woe to the inhabitants of the earth and the sea (Revelation 12:12)? Let's now look at the two beasts instrumental in those woes, one rising from the sea and the other from the earth, in Revelation 13.

The Beast from the Sea

Revelation 13:1 And I stood upon the sand of the sea, and saw a beast rise up out of the sea, having seven heads and ten horns, and upon his horns ten crowns, and upon his heads the name of blasphemy.

As we have already seen, a beast represents a demon-influenced human government that persecutes the people of God. John was literally on the Isle of Patmos in the Mediterranean Sea. The sea pictures peoples, multitudes, nations, and tongues (Revelation 17:15). Pagan Rome is a blasphemous system descending from Babylon, and is also symbolic of similar evils in other parts of the world.

The sea and abyss are two ways of describing where the beast arises from. The seven heads are explained later as seven mountains and also seven kings (Revelation 17:9-10). The ten horns are explained later as kings in waiting, who have not yet received a kingdom

(Revelation 17:12). They are subordinate kings.

Revelation 13:2 And the beast which I saw was like unto a leopard, and his feet were as the feet of a bear, and his mouth as the mouth of a lion: and the dragon gave him his power, and his seat, and great authority.

In the succession of blasphemous kingdoms from Daniel's prophecy, this Roman beast aligns itself with the predatory beasts which picture the preceding kingdoms, Babylon, Medo-Persia and Greece.

Revelation 13:3 And I saw one of his heads as it were wounded to death; and his deadly wound was healed: and all the world wondered after the beast.

Perhaps this is referring to a revival of pagan Rome, a resurrection.

Revelation 13:4 And they worshipped the dragon which gave power unto the beast: and they worshipped the beast, saying, Who is like unto the beast? who is able to make war with him?

Politicians and governments like to play God. Who is like the beast is reminiscent of words used to worship God alone (Exodus 15:11).

Revelation 13:5 And there was given unto him a mouth speaking great things and blasphemies; and power was given unto him to continue forty and two months.

Again we see the familiar period, time-limiting this secular power (Daniel 7:25; 12:7).

Revelation 13:6 And he opened his mouth in blasphemy against God, to blaspheme his name, and his tabernacle, [and] them that dwell in heaven.

The last "and" is not there in Greek, and so it should read, "his tabernacle, them that dwell in heaven." The Word of God became flesh and tabernacled with us (John 1:14) as God had tabernacled or tented with ancient Israel (Exodus 33:7). The tent of meeting became the temple. Today, the people of God are that temple (2 Corinthians 6:16).

Revelation 13:7 And it was given unto him to make war with the saints, and to overcome them: and power was given him over all kindreds, and tongues, and nations.

This arrogant anti-Christian world political power may overcome human lives but never the faith of those who endure to the end.

Revelation 13:8 And all that dwell upon the earth shall worship him, whose names are not written in the book of life of the Lamb slain from the foundation of the world.

Worship here means to fawn or kiss the ground. The fawning adoration of politicians and worldly solutions is worshipping the hidden power of the devil.

Revelation 13:9 If any man have an ear, let him hear.

This means to pay particular attention to the message.

Revelation 13:10 He that leadeth into captivity shall go into captivity: he that killeth with the sword must be killed with the sword. Here is the patience and the faith of the saints.

This is patience indeed, to suffer with endurance under anti-Christian governments and to know that God will ultimately punish them.

The Beast from the Earth

Revelation 13:11 And I beheld another beast coming up out of the earth; and he had two horns like a lamb, and he spake as a dragon.

This next beast looks like an innocent lamb, like Christ, but speaks like a dragon. His words betray him. Like a false prophet, this lamb is the opposite of what it seems (Revelation 16:13, 19:20, 20:10).

Revelation 13:12 And he exerciseth all the power of the first beast before him, and causeth the earth and them which dwell therein to worship the first beast, whose deadly wound was healed.

This false lamb exercises political power and incites the pagan worship of a worldly human government.

Revelation 13:13 And he doeth great wonders, so that he maketh fire come down from heaven on the earth in the sight of men,

Like the false prophets of old, they are to be judged by their words, not their ability to perform miracles (Deuteronomy 13).

Revelation 13:14 And deceiveth them that dwell on the earth by the means of those miracles which he had power to do in the sight of the beast; saying to them that dwell on the earth, that they should make an image to the beast, which had the wound by a sword, and did live.

The words of this false prophet, like others before him, are to incite idolatry.

Revelation 13:15 And he had power to give life unto the image of the beast, that the image of the beast should both speak, and cause that as many as would not worship the image of the beast should be killed.

Miracles surrounding religious statues mean nothing, when used to enforce bowing down to those statues and death threats. The worship of human leadership exists in both dictatorships and democracies even today.

Revelation 13:16 And he causeth all, both small and great, rich and poor, free and bond, to receive a mark in their right hand, or in their foreheads:

This expression comes from the Old Testament where the law and the words of God are to be a sign or mark in the hands and between the eyes, or in the foreheads, that is in our thoughts and deeds (Exodus 13:9; Exodus 13:16; Deuteronomy 6:8; Deuteronomy 11:18). Perhaps this includes a literal mark, as Paul bore some bodily marks of his suffering for Christ (Galatians 6:17), but more importantly it contrasts the seal of the beast with the seal of God.

The law is written in the minds (foreheads) and hearts of Christians (Jeremiah 31:33; Romans 2:15; Hebrews 8:10; Hebrews 10:16) and we are sealed by the Holy Spirit (2 Corinthians 1:22; Ephesians 1:13; Ephesians 4:30). We are either sealed with the mark of the beast, worshipping this world's systems, or sealed with the Holy Spirit, worshipping God alone.

Revelation 13:17 And that no man might buy or sell, save he that had the mark, or the name of the beast, or the number of his name.

As in Thyatira, where one could not buy or sell if one did not offer meat to the god of the guild representing your profession, so people will not be allowed to trade and make a living if they refuse beast worship.

Revelation 13:18 Here is wisdom. Let him that hath understanding count the number of the beast: for it is the number of a man; and his number is Six hundred threescore and six.

First thing we must note about this number is that it is the number of a man, like Nero and others down through history who have acted like him. Using alphabets which have letters doubling as numbers, this has been associated with the names of various world leaders over time.

The political and religious beasts of this world want us to worship them and their worldly governments supported by false religion disguised as a lamb, but speaking as a dragon. The true Christian sees through these falsehoods and worships God alone.

Revelation 14 - The Grapes of Wrath

Let's now look at several events surrounding the Lamb, the 144,000 and the hour of judgment in Revelation 14.

The Lamb and the 144,000

Revelation 14:1 And I looked, and, lo, a Lamb stood on the mount Sion, and with him an hundred forty and four thousand, having his Father's name written in their foreheads.

This is the same group revealed in Revelation 7, and seems to be symbolic Israel rather than physical Israel. Their identifying mark is the opposite of the mark of the beast, God the Father's name in their foreheads. Why is the innumerable multitude not mentioned? Perhaps this reveals the 144,000 as holding special positions in eternity.

Revelation 14:2 And I heard a voice from heaven, as the voice of many waters, and as the voice of a great thunder: and I heard the voice of harpers harping with their harps:

This reminds us of a voice from heaven at Christ's baptism. But here the voice is echoed by many.

Revelation 14:3 And they sung as it were a new song before the throne, and before the four beasts, and the elders: and no man could learn that song but the hundred and forty and four thousand, which were redeemed from the earth.

This is a new song and exclusively sung by them. Who are they?

Revelation 14:4 These are they which were not defiled with women; for they are virgins. These are they which follow the Lamb whithersoever he goeth. These were redeemed from among men, being the firstfruits unto God and to the Lamb.

Using the term firstfruits implies a special group and that others will also be saved but as second fruits. Sexual defilement here is related to the false religion of the whore of Babylon. By contrast, sexual purity marks all true Christians, as does its spiritual application, freedom from idolatry.

Revelation 14:5 And in their mouth was found no guile: for they are without fault before the throne of God.

No guile here refers to no lie. Idolatry is worshiping a lie. These are sincere, worshiping in spirit and truthful reality (John 4:24). Without fault means "blameless" (NIV, ESV, NASB) cleansed by the washing of water with the word (Ephesians 5:26-27). Only Jesus is able to make us stand blameless before the presence of His glory (Jude 24).

Angelic Announcements

Revelation 14:6 And I saw another angel fly in the midst of heaven, having the everlasting gospel to preach unto them that dwell on the earth, and to every nation, and kindred, and tongue, and people,

This is the first of several angels carrying a vital message.

Revelation 14:7 Saying with a loud voice, Fear God, and give glory to him; for the hour of his judgment is come: and worship him that made heaven, and earth, and the sea, and the fountains of waters.

Rather than being in terror of the beast and worldly powers, we should fear God, which involves a deep reverence of Him. Judgment day, a topic often avoided by those who love to preach "smooth things," is here connected with the good news, as the saints glorify God, because in Jesus we can have success on judgment day.

Revelation 14:8 And there followed another angel, saying, Babylon is fallen, is fallen, that great city, because she made all nations drink of the wine of the wrath of her fornication.

The second of these angels brings his assigned message. The descendant of Babylon was pagan Rome, picturing all governments that persecute Christians. All nations have been driven mad, corrupted by a worldly system of greed and oppression inherited from ancient Babylon (Jeremiah 51:7).

Revelation 14:9 And the third angel followed them, saying with a loud voice, If any man worship the beast and his image, and receive his mark in his forehead, or in his hand,

The third angel's announcement includes the word "receive" which implies that receiving the sign, badge of servitude, or mark of the beast is voluntary.

Revelation 14:10 The same shall drink of the wine of the wrath of God, which is poured out without mixture into the cup of his indignation; and he shall be tormented with fire and brimstone in the presence of the holy angels, and in the presence of the Lamb:

The wine of God's anger is not watered down. It pictures God's intense anger which contrasts with the often casual and accepting attitudes of society towards sin. There is no avoiding the fact that the angels and Jesus will oversee this punishment.

Revelation 14:11 And the smoke of their torment ascendeth up for ever and ever: and they have no rest day nor night, who worship the beast and his image, and whosoever receiveth the mark of his name.

In contrast with verse 13 and the eternal rest which the saints experience, there is no rest for the unrepentant worshipers of this world and its ways.

Revelation 14:12 Here is the patience of the saints: here are they that keep the commandments of God, and the faith of Jesus.

Christians keep the spiritual application of the commandments of God, not in a legalistic, letter-of-the-law manner as Paul was inspired to correct among the Galatians, but in the Spirit which gives life. This spirit-of-the-law obedience is coupled with faith in Jesus.

Revelation 14:13 And I heard a voice from heaven saying unto me, Write, Blessed are the dead which die in the Lord from henceforth: Yea, saith the Spirit, that they may rest from their labours; and their works do follow them.

Contrasted with the unrepentant, these are granted rest as they die in the Lord.

Revelation 14:14 And I looked, and behold a white cloud, and upon the cloud one sat like unto the Son of man, having on his head a golden crown, and in his hand a sharp sickle.

Jesus' ascension and return involve Him on a cloud (Acts 1:9-11; Matthew 24:30). The sickle pictures a hooked knife used in harvesting grapes.

The Time to Reap

Revelation 14:15 And another angel came out of the temple, crying with a loud voice to him that sat on the cloud, Thrust in thy sickle, and reap: for the time is come for thee to reap; for the harvest of the earth is ripe.

Now a fourth angel like an announcer, has a word of encouragement supporting our Lord and His next task.

Revelation 14:16 And he that sat on the cloud thrust in his sickle on the earth; and the earth was reaped.

We are reminded that the harvest is plentiful, that wheat and weeds grow together, and that the fields are already ripe for harvest (Matthew 9:37; Matthew 13:30; John 4:35). The one slight difference here is a grape harvest rather than a wheat harvest, though there is some overlap in meaning.

Revelation 14:17 And another angel came out of the temple which is in heaven, he also having a sharp sickle.

Now a fifth angel appears and his role is to join in the harvest with a sickle of his own.

Revelation 14:18 And another angel came out from the altar, which had power over fire; and cried with a loud cry to him that had the sharp sickle, saying, Thrust in thy sharp sickle, and gather the clusters of the vine of the earth; for her grapes are fully ripe.

Now a sixth angel shouts encouraging the fifth to thrust in his vineyard reaping hook. The harvest is ready and reminds us of Jesus' words during His earthly ministry (Matthew 9:35-38).

Revelation 14:19 And the angel thrust in his sickle into the earth, and gathered the vine of the earth, and cast it into the great winepress of the wrath of God.

In winemaking, the first order of duty is to crush the grapes harvested from the vines producing fresh grape juice. This winepress is described as God's wrath, picturing the final destruction of the wicked.

Revelation 14:20 And the winepress was trodden without the city, and blood came out of the winepress, even unto the horse bridles, by the space of a thousand and six hundred furlongs.

The fresh-squeezed grape juice pictures the blood of the wicked, shed in a great slaughter, a lake of blood 1600 stadia, about 180 miles or 300 kilometers across.

Unlike our society, God takes sin deadly seriously, because He knows that its end result is eternal suffering for all involved. He cannot and will not tolerate that which only destroys.

Revelation 15 - 7 Last Plagues

Let's look at an introduction to the judgment and the seven last plagues in Revelation 15.

Revelation 15:1 And I saw another sign in heaven, great and marvellous, seven angels having the seven last plagues; for in them is filled up the wrath of God.

These remind us of the plagues of Egypt directed against the unrepentant. They are blows, wounds or a flogging of punishment.

Revelation 15:2 And I saw as it were a sea of glass mingled with fire: and them that had gotten the victory over the beast, and over his image, and over his mark, and over the number of his name, stand on the sea of glass, having the harps of God.

This may be the same sea of glass seen in heaven (Revelation 4:6). It may be mingled with the fire of judgment.

Revelation 15:3 And they sing the song of Moses the servant of God, and the song of the Lamb, saying, Great and marvellous are thy works, Lord God Almighty; just and true are thy ways, thou King of saints.

The Song of Moses was a victory song over Egypt (Exodus 15:1-19). The addition of the Lamb to the title of this song means it is either a new song or the Lamb is now understood as the fulfillment in a new Exodus or both. The Exodus was an earlier victory over slavery to sin and oppressive human governments.

Revelation 15:4 Who shall not fear thee, O Lord, and glorify thy name? for thou only art holy: for all nations shall come and worship before thee; for thy judgments are made manifest.

With these words the Song of Moses becomes complete as a song of Christ's redemption.

Revelation 15:5 And after that I looked, and, behold, the temple of the tabernacle of the testimony in heaven was opened:

This refers to the holy of holies which was erected as a witness to God's presence. Here it refers to its heavenly reality.

Revelation 15:6 And the seven angels came out of the temple, having the seven plagues, clothed in pure and white linen, and having their breasts girded with golden girdles.

The duties of angels are many. The 7 punishments are carried out by duly appointed angels. Pure white or bright linen symbolizes righteousness. Breasts or chests clothed in gold may be similar to the ephod worn as priestly attire by Aaron and his sons (Exodus 28:8).

Revelation 15:7 And one of the four beasts gave unto the seven angels seven golden vials full of the wrath of God, who liveth for ever and ever.

This reveals heaven's full involvement in the punishment to come, a thought that liberals and universalists have difficulty explaining.

Revelation 15:8 And the temple was filled with smoke from the glory of God, and from his power; and no man was able to enter into the temple, till the seven plagues of the seven angels were fulfilled.

This particular smoke is not associated with the incense and our prayers directly but with the glory of God, like at Mount Sinai (Exodus 19:18) and in the temple (Isaiah 4:5; Isaiah 6:4). These plagues are punishment upon the belligerently unrepentant.

God will not allow destructive sin to ruin the lives of all it touches for very much longer. The unrepentant must and will be punished.

Revelation 16 - God's Wrath

We are tempted to only want smooth things preached to us, yet that would ignore the whole counsel of God, including some things we might rather avoid. Let's now look at the seven bowls or vials of God's wrath and begin to understand why God is angry with sin, in Revelation 16.

Revelation 16:1 And I heard a great voice out of the temple saying to the seven angels, Go your ways, and pour out the vials of the wrath of God upon the earth.

Whose is the great voice? We are not told. The trumpets and vials (bowls) have this in common, the last three are worse than the first four. Why is God's anger aroused? It is against ungodliness, unrighteousness and suppression of truth (Romans 1:18).

God's wrath is also against those who mock His messengers (2 Chronicles 36:16). It was against Israel for not believing God, nor trusting His salvation (Psalm 78:21-31). It is still because of unbelief (John 3:36). It is because of hard and unrepentant hearts (Romans 2:5). It is because of things like sexual immorality, impurity, evil desires, and greed, which is idolatry (Ephesians 5:5-7; Colossians 3:5-7).

1st Vial

Revelation 16:2 And the first went, and poured out his vial upon the earth; and there fell a noisome and grievous sore upon the men which had the mark of the beast, and upon them which worshipped his image.

Much like Job's ulcers or boils this could refer to physical pain, but also spiritual affliction.

2nd Vial

Revelation 16:3 And the second angel poured out his vial upon the sea; and it became as the blood of a dead man: and every living soul died in the sea.

This seems similar to the plague in ancient Egypt, where the fish in the river died (Exodus 7:20-21). In the sea, every living thing dies.

3rd Vial

Revelation 16:4-7 And the third angel poured out his vial upon the rivers and fountains of waters; and they became blood. And I heard the angel of the waters say, Thou art righteous, O Lord, which art, and wast, and shalt be, because thou hast judged thus. For they have shed the blood of saints and prophets, and thou hast given them blood to drink; for they are worthy. And I heard another out of the altar say, Even so, Lord God Almighty, true and righteous are thy judgments.

The plague is extended to the water sources. This angel praises God for His judgment, unlike some who may falsely label God's judgment as spiritual abuse. The angels have witnessed how human sin has hurt humanity since the beginning, and because of their experience seeing human misery throughout history, they know that God's judgment is right and good.

Is God vengeful? Not in a human sense. The Godly purpose would be to teach the kind of lesson that only the one can teach, who can take and also give life back. It's as if God is saying this is what it is like to have blood to the full. Will they learn?

In contrast to much human criticism of God's judgments, those who really know are those who have witnessed the depravity of the entirety of human history, and they understand how true and righteous His judgments really are.

4th Vial

Revelation 16:8-9 And the fourth angel poured out his vial upon the sun; and power was given unto him to scorch men with fire. And men were scorched with great heat, and blasphemed the name of God, which hath power over these plagues: and they repented not to give him glory.

Is this global warming, a military power scorching beast worshipers or something else? There has been much wild speculation down through history. One thing is certain, this punishment does not produce the desired result, but men continue blaspheming God and do not have a change of heart to give Him glory.

5th Vial

Revelation 16:10-11 And the fifth angel poured out his vial upon the seat of the beast; and his kingdom was full of darkness; and they gnawed their tongues for pain, And blasphemed the God of heaven because of their pains and their sores, and repented not of their deeds.

Darkness with pain is also similar to one of the Egyptian plagues (Exodus 10:21-22), and the result is similarly disappointing. Men still refuse to repent.

6th Vial

Revelation 16:12-14 And the sixth angel poured out his vial upon the great river Euphrates; and the water thereof was dried up, that the way of the kings of the east might be prepared. And I saw three unclean spirits like frogs come out of the mouth of the dragon, and out of the mouth of the beast, and out of the mouth of the false prophet. For they are the spirits of devils, working miracles, which go forth unto the kings of the earth and of the whole world, to gather them to the battle of that great day of God Almighty.

Three unclean spirits represent Christianity's foes of the demonic world, the political world and counterfeit religion. These gather anti-Christian world leaders to the battle of the great day.

Revelation 16:15-16 Behold, I come as a thief. Blessed is he that watcheth, and keepeth his garments, lest he walk naked, and they see his shame. And he gathered them together into a place called in the Hebrew tongue Armageddon.

This describes a diligent night watch, who keeps his clothes on. This watcher is clothed in the righteousness of faith (Philippians 3:9). This location of the battle of the great day of God Almighty is either literal or symbolic or both. It literally describes the hill of Megiddo, or Tel-Megiddo which overlooks the Valley of Jezreel, where many historic battles took place, and is symbolic of the final defeat of evil.

7th Vial

Revelation 16:17 And the seventh angel poured out his vial into the air; and there came a great voice out of the temple of heaven, from the throne, saying, It is done.

It is done. The plagues are finished.

Revelation 16:18 And there were voices, and thunders, and lightnings; and there was a great earthquake, such as was not since men were upon the earth, so mighty an earthquake, and so great.

An unprecedented great earthquake occurs (Haggai 2:6; Hebrews 12:26-27).

Revelation 16:19 And the great city was divided into three parts, and the cities of the nations fell: and great Babylon came in remembrance before God, to give unto her the cup of the wine of the fierceness of his wrath.

Which is the great city? It is not mentioned. Speculation abounds that it may be Rome, Babylon or Jerusalem. In the next chapter we are introduced to the great whore who has the name of Babylon written on her forehead. However, let's not become dogmatic about it or sidetracked by speculation. The meaning is found in what is clear. What is clear is that God is angry with any civilization that sets itself against Him.

Revelation 16:20 And every island fled away, and the mountains were not found.

Even the isolated islands and mountain retreats of this evil system are destroyed.

Revelation 16:21 And there fell upon men a great hail out of heaven, every stone about the weight of a talent: and men blasphemed God because of the plague of the hail; for the plague thereof was exceeding great.

These hailstones weigh about 75 pounds, 35 kilograms each. The incredible destruction does not have its desired effect. Stubborn hearts remain unrepentant, even in death.

Evil brings its own self-destruction. Sin hurts us and our families first, and destroys everything it touches. God's destruction of all evil is for humanity's own good, but those enslaved to sin find it hard to let go. The last plagues are upon those who refuse to repent. We who have repented need not fear God's wrath. In the end, those on God's side win.

Revelation 17 - the Great Harlot

Let's now look at the prophecy of the mother of harlots and of the abominations of the earth, the scarlet woman in Revelation 17.

Revelation 17:1 And there came one of the seven angels which had the seven vials, and talked with me, saying unto me, Come hither; I will shew unto thee the judgment of the great whore that sitteth upon many waters:

Spiritual adultery is betraying the true God (Hosea 1:2; Jeremiah 3:6-8). It's too easy to point to another church and pretend that doing so makes us without sin. Yet, all who profess true religion, but are unfaithful to God and His Word, play the whore. When any of us prioritizes empty human traditions or sinful worldly values over the Word of God, we are committing spiritual adultery.

Revelation 17:2 With whom the kings of the earth have committed fornication, and the inhabitants of the earth have been made drunk with the wine of her fornication.

The church is pictured as a woman and Jerusalem above is the mother of us all. This woman may thus be a counterfeit church or even the tares among the wheat within the church. Fornication is another way of saying spiritual adultery. False religion is often used to legitimize corrupt world leaders and crowds become drunk with populist mass hysteria and false ideals.

Revelation 17:3 So he carried me away in the spirit into the wilderness: and I saw a woman sit upon a scarlet coloured beast, full of names of blasphemy, having seven heads and ten horns.

This woman rides the beast that was earlier revealed as an antichristian government (Revelation 13). Now it looks a little different as more details emerge. It is crimson, the color of blood. Riding the beast indicates some kind of mutual relationship between false religion and evil government.

Revelation 17:4 And the woman was arrayed in purple and scarlet colour, and decked with gold and precious stones and pearls, having a golden cup in her hand full of abominations and filthiness of her fornication:

She is rich and royal and filthy with sin and carries what looks like a communion cup but full of abominations.

Revelation 17:5 And upon her forehead was a name written, Mystery, Babylon The Great, The

Mother Of Harlots And Abominations Of The Earth.

She is identified as associated with the corruption of ancient Babylon and its system of human exploitation and oppression. This is not the mystery of the wisdom of God or godliness (1 Corinthians 2:7; 1 Timothy 3:16). It is the mystery of lawlessness or iniquity (2 Thessalonians 2:6-12).

Revelation 17:6 And I saw the woman drunken with the blood of the saints, and with the blood of the martyrs of Jesus: and when I saw her, I wondered with great admiration.

The woman of Revelation 12 is persecuted. This woman persecutes. Christianity is the most persecuted religion in the world, most intensely in over sixty countries from north Africa to Asia. Tens of thousands are killed every year and thousands are imprisoned.

Revelation 17:7 And the angel said unto me, Wherefore didst thou marvel? I will tell thee the mystery of the woman, and of the beast that carrieth her, which hath the seven heads and ten horns.

An angel offers to reveal the mystery.

Revelation 17:8 The beast that thou sawest was, and is not; and shall ascend out of the bottomless pit, and go into perdition: and they that dwell on the earth shall wonder, whose names were not written in the book of life from the foundation of the world, when they behold the beast that was, and is not, and yet is.

The tyrannical antichristian empire that was, and failed, will again rise. Most understand this to be a revival of a murderous, pagan Roman system, which was itself a revival of an even more ancient Babylonian system. Those who have never been written into the book of life will be easily deceived.

Revelation 17:9 And here is the mind which hath wisdom. The seven heads are seven mountains, on which the woman sitteth.

The seven mountains may refer to the seven hills of ancient Rome or seven kings that rule.

Revelation 17:10 And there are seven kings: five are fallen, and one is, and the other is not yet come; and when he cometh, he must continue a short space.

Five previous world empires, one at the time of writing was Rome and the other is assumed to be a king not yet in existence.

Revelation 17:11 And the beast that was, and is not, even he is the eighth, and is of the seven, and goeth into perdition.

The beast is described here as being "of" the same evil spirit as the seven preceding oppressive dictatorships.

Revelation 17:12 And the ten horns which thou sawest are ten kings, which have received no kingdom as yet; but receive power as kings one hour with the beast.

These kings in waiting join with the beast in a federation of ten states.

Revelation 17:13 These have one mind, and shall give their power and strength unto the beast.

These kings are subservient.

Revelation 17:14 These shall make war with the Lamb, and the Lamb shall overcome them: for he is Lord of lords, and King of kings: and they that are with him are called, and chosen, and faithful.

Christianity has always been engaged in spiritual warfare. However, this is more specifically the battle of the great day of the Lord.

Revelation 17:15 And he saith unto me, The waters which thou sawest, where the whore sitteth, are peoples, and multitudes, and nations, and tongues.

Here is one of those keys to the prophecy.

Revelation 17:16 And the ten horns which thou sawest upon the beast, these shall hate the whore, and shall make her desolate and naked, and shall eat her flesh, and burn her with fire.

In the end, the alliance between the whore of Babylon and these kings will fail.

Revelation 17:17 For God hath put in their hearts to fulfil his will, and to agree, and give their kingdom unto the beast, until the words of God shall be fulfilled.

The alliance will only last as long as God wills.

Revelation 17:18 And the woman which thou sawest is that great city, which reigneth over the kings of the earth.

This is who Babylon really is, a descendant of that idolatrous system which has corrupted the whole world.

The whole world must choose between two ways, the way of Babylon and the way of God. Do we worship this antichristian world and its ways or is our allegiance to God and the kingdom of heaven?

Revelation 18 - Babylon's Fall

Let's now take a look at the fall of Babylon, the end of a corrupt world political and religious system, in Revelation 18.

Revelation 18:1 And after these things I saw another angel come down from heaven, having great power; and the earth was lightened with his glory.

This important event, the close of a chapter of mixed religious and political corruption, is delegated to another angel.

Revelation 18:2 And he cried mightily with a strong voice, saying, Babylon the great is fallen, is fallen, and is become the habitation of devils, and the hold of every foul spirit, and a cage of every unclean and hateful bird.

The outward trappings of this corrupt system are gone and what is at the heart of it lies exposed for all to see.

Revelation 18:3 For all nations have drunk of the wine of the wrath of her fornication, and the kings of the earth have committed fornication with her, and the merchants of the earth are waxed rich through the abundance of her delicacies.

Politicians and merchants of all nations have partaken of the corruption of this horrid system.

Revelation 18:4 And I heard another voice from heaven, saying, Come out of her, my people, that ye be not partakers of her sins, and that ye receive not of her plagues.

"Come out of her" is a mandate to the church. Though we must live in this world, we do not partake of its corrupt politics and business practices.

Revelation 18:5 For her sins have reached unto heaven, and God hath remembered her iniquities.

The Holy Spirit has inspired the Holy Scriptures, which will teach any Christian who is submissive to God, what is right and wrong. In this manner, the Scriptures are self-correcting of all heresies and apostasies that may creep into our midst, bringing periodic Reformation to those who are willing.

Revelation 18:6 Reward her even as she rewarded you, and double unto her double according to her works: in the cup which she hath filled fill to her double.

The ills that this Babylonian system have brought upon the world will be visited upon her double.

Revelation 18:7 How much she hath glorified herself, and lived deliciously, so much torment and sorrow give her: for she saith in her heart, I sit a queen, and am no widow, and shall see no sorrow.

Christians who are in tune with the Holy Spirit will instantly recognize and reject such bragging and narcissistic self-glorification.

Revelation 18:8 Therefore shall her plagues come in one day, death, and mourning, and famine; and she shall be utterly burned with fire: for strong is the Lord God who judgeth her.

Jesus tells us not to judge or condemn, yet in the same chapter not to give what is holy to those who would only trample it down, and to beware of false prophets (Matthew 7). So, we must not judge wrongly but we must judge or discern between right and wrong. Here we see that God will ultimately judge all evil.

Revelation 18:9 And the kings of the earth, who have committed fornication and lived deliciously with her, shall bewail her, and lament for her, when they shall see the smoke of her burning,

When this world's self-destructive and oppressive system ultimately ends, those who have profited from it will be very sad.

Revelation 18:10 Standing afar off for the fear of her torment, saying, Alas, alas that great city Babylon, that mighty city! for in one hour is thy judgment come.

They will be shocked that her destruction came about so suddenly and will stand back in case Babylon's destruction also consumes them.

Revelation 18:11 And the merchants of the earth shall weep and mourn over her; for no man buyeth their merchandise any more:

God reveals in the parable of the talents (Matthew 25:14-30) that there is a righteous form of capitalism, from whom much is given, much is expected. Babylon is a system of idolatrous greed, capitalism without any love of neighbor.

Revelation 18:12 The merchandise of gold, and silver, and precious stones, and of pearls, and fine linen, and purple, and silk, and scarlet, and all thyine wood, and all manner vessels of ivory, and all manner vessels of most precious wood, and of brass, and iron, and marble,

Babylon is a very wealthy system for those who profit from it, but a very oppressive system, especially hard on those who love God.

Revelation 18:13 And cinnamon, and odours, and ointments, and frankincense, and wine, and oil, and fine flour, and wheat, and beasts, and sheep, and horses, and chariots, and slaves, and souls of men.

Slaves? We must not believe for a second that the days of slavery are over. It still exists and it will return.

Revelation 18:14 And the fruits that thy soul lusted after are departed from thee, and all things which were dainty and goodly are departed from thee, and thou shalt find them no more at all.

Babylon is an empty shell. Her fancy delicacies are gone.

Revelation 18:15 The merchants of these things, which were made rich by her, shall stand afar off for the fear of her torment, weeping and wailing,

This is the end of all unrighteous forms of capitalism, whereby men are made slaves, the environment is ruined and Christians are oppressed.

Revelation 18:16 And saying, Alas, alas that great city, that was clothed in fine linen, and purple, and scarlet, and decked with gold, and precious stones, and pearls!

When men say that God has blessed their land with wealth, we ought to ask if that wealth has been gotten with Babylonian systems, on the backs of oppressed people, in other lands or at home, because all countries refuse to face their own sins.

Revelation 18:17 For in one hour so great riches is come to nought. And every shipmaster, and all the company in ships, and sailors, and as many as trade by sea, stood afar off,

When we thank God for the riches of our nation, let's ask ourselves if we would willingly give it all up so that others may eat today, drink good water and have shelter.

Revelation 18:18 And cried when they saw the smoke of her burning, saying, What city is like unto this great city!

When we brag that ours is the greatest nation, the best of this or that, are we actually admitting that we are a part of this corrupt Babylonian system?

Revelation 18:19 And they cast dust on their heads, and cried, weeping and wailing, saying, Alas, alas that great city, wherein were made rich all that had ships in the sea by reason of her costliness! for in one hour is she made desolate.

Let's never forget that this system will end in one hour.

Revelation 18:20 Rejoice over her, thou heaven, and ye holy apostles and prophets; for God hath avenged you on her.

How many of us will rejoice when this world's systems fall?

Revelation 18:21 And a mighty angel took up a stone like a great millstone, and cast it into the sea, saying, Thus with violence shall that great city Babylon be thrown down, and shall be found no more at all.

Using a rock as a demonstration, and with a large splash Babylon is gone.

Revelation 18:22 And the voice of harpers, and musicians, and of pipers, and trumpeters, shall be heard no more at all in thee; and no craftsman, of whatsoever craft he be, shall be found any more in thee; and the sound of a millstone shall be heard no more at all in thee;

The sights and sounds of unethical world entertainment, manufacturing and agricultural practices will be no more.

Revelation 18:23 And the light of a candle shall shine no more at all in thee; and the voice of the bridegroom and of the bride shall be heard no more at all in thee: for thy merchants were the great men of the earth; for by thy sorceries were all nations deceived.

Mixing of merchandising and witchcraft will no longer deceive the nations.

Revelation 18:24 And in her was found the blood of prophets, and of saints, and of all that were slain upon the earth.

The real cost of a corrupt religious, political, manufacturing, and merchandising system is the high cost of human lives and especially those who dare preach the Word of God.

Heaven is not against righteous capitalism, the buying and selling of goods done in love for God and neighbor. However, that form of self-destructive capitalism inherited from ancient

Babylon is often an excuse for idolatrous greed, mercilessly devouring the poor and suppressing the messengers of Divine truth. That system is about to die.

Revelation 19 - Alleluia

Now begins the rejoicing. The good news for a grieving world is near. Revelation 19 begins with praise for God and joy that this world's corrupt ways, symbolically referred to as Babylon and the beast, have finally ended.

Revelation 19:1 And after these things I heard a great voice of much people in heaven, saying, Alleluia; Salvation, and glory, and honour, and power, unto the Lord our God:

What a shout of joy! The evils of this world are finally ending. Humanity has tried every variety of political, religious and scientific method, and none brought the salvation available only in God. Rather than a polluted world caused by human mismanagement, we have glory. Rather than the honor of scoundrels and dishonor of the weak, true honor is given to God, who only has the power to bring salvation to the world.

Revelation 19:2 For true and righteous are his judgments: for he hath judged the great whore, which did corrupt the earth with her fornication, and hath avenged the blood of his servants at her hand.

No longer will there be the miscarriage of justice, but God's righteous judgments. Fair punishment will come to a corrupt Babylonian system, apostate religion, blood-guilty oppression and one-sided injustice.

Revelation 19:3 And again they said, Alleluia And her smoke rose up for ever and ever.

Babylon's smoke "rises" up forever, similar to a prophecy of the destruction of Edom (Isaiah 34:9-10), which was understood by Jews as symbolic of their oppressors, pagan Rome and its eventual destruction.

Revelation 19:4 And the four and twenty elders and the four beasts fell down and worshipped God that sat on the throne, saying, Amen; Alleluia.

God "sits" on the throne, present tense. The angels at God's throne join in this anthem of praise.

Revelation 19:5 And a voice came out of the throne, saying, Praise our God, all ye his servants, and ye that fear him, both small and great.

A voice invites the church to a time of praise.

Revelation 19:6 And I heard as it were the voice of a great multitude, and as the voice of many waters, and as the voice of mighty thunderings, saying, Alleluia: for the Lord God omnipotent reigneth.

All heaven and all saints join in praise of our God. This is a time of great joy for all, humanity and angels alike.

Revelation 19:7 Let us be glad and rejoice, and give honour to him: for the marriage of the Lamb is come, and his wife hath made herself ready.

The marriage of Christ to His bride the church is consummated. This metaphor of a marriage covenant between Savior and church, seems to be pictured in various stages throughout history and this is the final culmination.

Revelation 19:8 And to her was granted that she should be arrayed in fine linen, clean and white: for the fine linen is the righteousness of saints.

As white symbolizes purity in many cultures, so too does it symbolize the righteousness of the church, through faith in Jesus Christ (Romans 3:22; 4:5; 4:9; 4:13; 10:6; 10:10; Galatians 3:6; 5:5; Philippians 3:9; Hebrews 11:7).

Revelation 19:9 And he saith unto me, Write, Blessed are they which are called unto the marriage supper of the Lamb. And he saith unto me, These are the true sayings of God.

The Lord's Supper is a small picture of this great marriage supper. Recall the parable of the wedding feast, whereby many were invited but refused to come (Matthew 22:1-14).

Revelation 19:10 And I fell at his feet to worship him. And he said unto me, See thou do it not: I am thy fellowservant, and of thy brethren that have the testimony of Jesus: worship God: for the testimony of Jesus is the spirit of prophecy.

This is a wonderful example of loyalty to God set by an angel, a fellow servant! Angels and men work together as servants of God. The spirit or purpose of prophecy is to make God's will known, and it is most fully known in Jesus.

The White Horse

Revelation 19:11 And I saw heaven opened, and behold a white horse; and he that sat upon him was called Faithful and True, and in righteousness he doth judge and make war.

No longer riding on the foal of a donkey (Matthew 21:1-7), but a white horse, Jesus comes to finally vanquish all evil, symbolized in the beast of antichristian governments, corrupt trade and the whore of counterfeit religion.

Revelation 19:12-13 His eyes were as a flame of fire, and on his head were many crowns; and he had a name written, that no man knew, but he himself. And he was clothed with a vesture dipped in blood: and his name is called The Word of God.

This is obviously Jesus. The phrase the Word of God means many things, the spoken Word, the written Word, the Gospel, but when personalized, it refers to Jesus (John 1:1-3, 14)

Revelation 19:14 And the armies which were in heaven followed him upon white horses, clothed in fine linen, white and clean.

Are there animals in heaven? Interesting! It seems that resurrected saints are part of that victorious army.

Revelation 19:15-16 And out of his mouth goeth a sharp sword, that with it he should smite the nations: and he shall rule them with a rod of iron: and he treadeth the winepress of the fierceness and wrath of Almighty God. And he hath on his vesture and on his thigh a name written, King Of Kings, And Lord Of Lords.

World peace can come by no other means than to put down all evil with strong rule (Psalm 2:9). This will not be a democracy, where the worldly will of the people decides what is right or wrong. On the other hand, by our actions, we do vote for or against Jesus' reign in our lives.

The reign of heaven will not be a self-serving kind of monarchy, where kings take from a peasant class and make them landless serfs. It will not be communism whereby party bosses become billionaires and ordinary people suffer in poverty. It will be divine rule by the only one qualified, with righteous justice for all.

Revelation 19:17-18 And I saw an angel standing in the sun; and he cried with a loud voice, saying to all the fowls that fly in the midst of heaven, Come and gather yourselves together unto the supper of the great God; That ye may eat the flesh of kings, and the flesh of captains, and the flesh of mighty men, and the flesh of horses, and of them that sit on them, and the flesh of all men, both free and bond, both small and great.

This is the end of all corrupt wordly systems symbolized by Babylon, whereby the powerful prey on the weak, and men seek only personal gain without love of neighbor. Instead, the birds will symbolically feed on them.

Revelation 19:19 And I saw the beast, and the kings of the earth, and their armies, gathered together to make war against him that sat on the horse, and against his army.

The antichristian instinct of those caught up in a worldly, Babylonian system of selfishness and greed, is to fight against God in one last ditch, futile effort to prevent the reign of Christ.

Revelation 19:20 And the beast was taken, and with him the false prophet that wrought miracles before him, with which he deceived them that had received the mark of the beast, and them that worshipped his image. These both were cast alive into a lake of fire burning with brimstone.

Antichristian politics, wealth gained through exploitation, abominations of the earth, and counterfeit religion will cease permanently, symbolized by them being cast into a volcanic lake of burning sulphur.

Revelation 19:21 And the remnant were slain with the sword of him that sat upon the horse, which sword proceeded out of his mouth: and all the fowls were filled with their flesh.

The sword is the Word of God, and symbolizes the criterion whereby their lives are judged. The word "remnant" is a hopeful description that at least some of them may finally repent and be converted (Romans 9:27; 11:5).

For those suffering around the world under oppressive governments, employers antagonistic to people of faith, abandonment by relatives, abuse from spouses and courts, and maltreatment in apostate churches, this gives hope of final justice. It requires a hope that endures. It requires a faith that stands strong. Those on the side of Christ will win, and a wonderful eternity awaits.

Revelation 20 - The Thousand Years

The time of world peace will finally come. Whether it is a literal or symbolic period of a thousand years is not as important as its arrival. It will be here at last, as described in Revelation 20.

Revelation 20:1 And I saw an angel come down from heaven, having the key of the bottomless pit and a great chain in his hand.

The ultimate cause of all world problems, the chief of rebellious angels will be dealt with by a powerful angel who has the key to the abyss, the place of restraint (2 Peter 2:4).

Revelation 20:2 And he laid hold on the dragon, that old serpent, which is the Devil, and Satan, and bound him a thousand years,

He is bound for a time, symbolized by a thousand years of peace, prevented from deceiving the world.

Revelation 20:3 And cast him into the bottomless pit, and shut him up, and set a seal upon him, that he should deceive the nations no more, till the thousand years should be fulfilled: and after that he must be loosed a little season.

Apocalyptic literature is symbolic. It is therefore not wise to be dogmatic whether the thousand years is literal or not. What is plain is that after this period of peace, the evil one will be allowed a short period to test humanity and its loyalty to God.

Revelation 20:4 And I saw thrones, and they sat upon them, and judgment was given unto them: and I saw the souls of them that were beheaded for the witness of Jesus, and for the word of God, and which had not worshipped the beast, neither his image, neither had received his mark upon their foreheads, or in their hands; and they lived and reigned with Christ a thousand years.

The resurrected saints are those who do not worship this world's ways, nor are marked in their thoughts or deeds by beastly world ideals, but the opposite, the sign of God, the seal of the Holy Spirit marks their lives. They will rule with Jesus.

Revelation 20:5 But the rest of the dead lived not again until the thousand years were finished. This is the first resurrection.

This points to the first and not the second resurrection. The righteous and unrighteous will be resurrected at different times. The first resurrection is to life, a thousand years before the second resurrection.

Revelation 20:6 Blessed and holy is he that hath part in the first resurrection: on such the second death hath no power, but they shall be priests of God and of Christ, and shall reign with him a thousand years.

This first resurrection of the saints takes place at Christ's return as the thousand years begin. They do not die again, by the death of the soul in eternal separation from God. One theory states that they will reign with Christ a thousand years "upon the surface of" the earth (Revelation 5:10). Another possible meaning is that they will reign "over" the earth, but from heaven.

Revelation 20:7 And when the thousand years are expired, Satan shall be loosed out of his prison, And shall go out to deceive the nations which are in the four quarters of the earth, Gog, and Magog, to gather them together to battle: the number of whom is as the sand of the sea.

At the end of this period of restraint and the resulting world peace, times of trouble are about to return from the four directions of the compass, symbolized by Gog and Magog, once ancient enemies of Israel (Ezekiel 38-39).

Revelation 20:9 And they went up on the breadth of the earth, and compassed the camp of the saints about, and the beloved city: and fire came down from God out of heaven, and devoured them.

This futile battle is similar to the evil angels who tried to invade heaven, utterly useless.

Revelation 20:10 And the devil that deceived them was cast into the lake of fire and brimstone, where the beast and the false prophet are, and shall be tormented day and night for ever and ever.

The good news at this point is that the devil is done, forever.

The Judgment

Revelation 20:11 And I saw a great white throne, and him that sat on it, from whose face the earth and the heaven fled away; and there was found no place for them.

This great white throne is elsewhere described as the throne of His glory (Matthew 25:31). This is a throne of pure, blinding judgment.

Revelation 20:12 And I saw the dead, small and great, stand before God; and the books were opened: and another book was opened, which is the book of life: and the dead were judged out of those things which were written in the books, according to their works.

What books? This is difficult for those who reject parts of the Bible that they do not like. If we are saved by faith, how can we be judged by works? We are saved BY faith, but saved FOR good works. Those who show no fruits of good works do not have a saving faith, because faith without works is dead (James 2:14-26).

Revelation 20:13 And the sea gave up the dead which were in it; and death and hell delivered up the dead which were in them: and they were judged every man according to their works.

What is meant by hell here? It is translated from the Greek word "Hades" which means the realm of the dead, and in this context, simply refers to the grave.

Revelation 20:14 And death and hell were cast into the lake of fire. This is the second death. And whosoever was not found written in the book of life was cast into the lake of fire.

Here is the definition of the second death. It is the lake of fire, symbolizing eternal separation of all not found in the book of life.

This is the only place in the Bible where the thousand years are mentioned. It is not wise to be overly dogmatic, taking it literally in a genre that is largely symbolic. It can be interesting to speculate, but what we DO know is that God is in control, He has a plan to save the world from sin, He will reward the faithful and punish the unrepentant.

Revelation 21 - New Heaven & Earth

Now the good news continues. After the defeat of all corruption and evil, a new heaven and a new earth are described in Revelation 21.

Revelation 21:1 And I saw a new heaven and a new earth: for the first heaven and the first earth were passed away; and there was no more sea.

Foretold by Isaiah (Isaiah 65:17), foreseen by Ezekiel (Ezekiel 40-48), and alluded to by Jesus (Matthew 19:28), all things will be new. Whether this means brand new or renewed during a symbolic thousand years of peace, remains an open question.

New Jerusalem

Revelation 21:2 And I John saw the holy city, new Jerusalem, coming down from God out of heaven, prepared as a bride adorned for her husband.

Jerusalem above is symbolic of our mother, the church (Galatians 4:26; Hebrews 12:22-24). She is populated by the saints. A significant hill in Jerusalem is mount Zion and also symbolizes the church (Hebrews 12:22-24). The church is the Bride of Christ (Matthew 25:1-13; 2 Corinthians 11:2; Ephesians 5:21-

24; Revelation 19:7-8). This Bride is not dressed for a worldly fashion parade, but for her husband.

Revelation 21:3 And I heard a great voice out of heaven saying, Behold, the tabernacle of God is with men, and he will dwell with them, and they shall be his people, and God himself shall be with them, and be their God.

When we speak of going to heaven when we die, we often overlook the time when heaven and earth will be one and God will dwell with men.

Revelation 21:4 And God shall wipe away all tears from their eyes; and there shall be no more death, neither sorrow, nor crying, neither shall there be any more pain: for the former things are passed away.

We may ask questions about lost loved ones, children who died in infancy and people groups whose ancestors died without even knowing about Jesus. There is plenty of speculation, but one thing is sure, that if there will be no more tears, there will be no more reason for tears. Beyond speculation, we don't know the answers, but we do know that God is a God of grace and mercy and His justice is righteous.

Revelation 21:5 And he that sat upon the throne said, Behold, I make all things new. And he said unto me, Write: for these words are true and faithful.

If anyone is in Christ, he is a new creation (2 Corinthians 5:17; Galatians 6:15).

Revelation 21:6 And he said unto me, It is done. I am Alpha and Omega, the beginning and the end. I will give unto him that is athirst of the fountain of the water of life freely.

The task of making all things new is finished and access to eternal life is still available to those who want it. One crucial task was done on the cross and that work is finished completely by this renewal. It is completed in the Lord's death, burial, resurrection, ascension return and renewal of heaven and earth.

Revelation 21:7 He that overcometh shall inherit all things; and I will be his God, and he shall be my son.

Cheap grace without a life of overcoming is not a Christian life. The "double cure" of forgiveness of our sins and the gift of the Holy Spirit (Acts 2:38-39) to make overcoming possible, is the Christian life.

Revelation 21:8 But the fearful, and unbelieving, and the abominable, and murderers, and whoremongers, and sorcerers, and idolaters, and all liars, shall have their part in the lake which burneth with fire and brimstone: which is the second death.

This list of sins begins with fearfulness. Fear is the opposite of faith. The second death results after a resurrection and is the final destination of all sinners. Some take this as a literal death, and others take it as eternal suffering that is like a death. Either way, there is a bad and a good eternity. Let's choose the good eternity.

Revelation 21:9 And there came unto me one of the seven angels which had the seven vials full of the seven last plagues, and talked with me, saying, Come hither, I will shew thee the bride, the Lamb's wife.

This pure woman is the bride of Christ, and is a contrast to counterfeit religion, apostasy and heresy.

Revelation 21:10 And he carried me away in the spirit to a great and high mountain, and shewed me that great city, the holy Jerusalem, descending out of heaven from God,

Zion is actually a small hill in historic Jerusalem, but the true church has the stature of a "great and high mountain" spiritually speaking. So many are redeemed in the church that they fill a whole city, new Jerusalem which will come down out of heaven.

Revelation 21:11 Having the glory of God: and her light was like unto a stone most precious, even like a jasper stone, clear as crystal;

The splendor or "kabowd" of God has been experienced before in the tabernacle and temple (Exodus 40:35; 1 Kings 8:11).

Revelation 21:12 And had a wall great and high, and had twelve gates, and at the gates twelve angels, and names written thereon, which are the names of the twelve tribes of the children of Israel:

New Jerusalem, the church, will have traffic in and out. The twelve gates signify the ancient stamp of physical Israel upon spiritual Israel, the church.

Revelation 21:13 On the east three gates; on the north three gates; on the south three gates; and on the west three gates.

As Israel camped in the wilderness, with three tribes on each point of the compass surrounding the tabernacle, so this echoes that arrangement.

Revelation 21:14 And the wall of the city had twelve foundations, and in them the names of the twelve apostles of the Lamb.

This echoes the description of the church "built on the foundation of the apostles and prophets, Jesus Christ Himself being the chief cornerstone" (Ephesians 2:19-22 NKJV).

Revelation 21:15 And he that talked with me had a golden reed to measure the city, and the gates thereof, and the wall thereof.

This is similar to an ancient vision of a new city and a new temple (Ezekiel 40).

Revelation 21:16 And the city lieth foursquare, and the length is as large as the breadth: and he measured the city with the reed, twelve thousand furlongs. The length and the breadth and the height of it are equal.

These symbolic measurements may picture perfection more than reality. The distance is 12,000 times the distance an ancient runner would run to win a race. We all run the Christian race to obtain our prize (1 Corinthians 9:24-27).

Revelation 21:17 And he measured the wall thereof, an hundred and forty and four cubits, according to the measure of a man, that is, of the angel.

Though this may be the height of the wall, it could also be its thickness.

Revelation 21:18 And the building of the wall of it was of jasper: and the city was pure gold, like unto clear glass.

The masonry of the wall was like a translucent stone or quartz, possibly red, brown or green.

Revelation 21:19-20 And the foundations of the wall of the city were garnished with all manner of precious stones. The first foundation was jasper; the second, sapphire; the third, a chalcedony; the fourth, an emerald; The fifth, sardonyx; the sixth, sardius; the seventh, chrysolyte; the eighth, beryl; the ninth, a topaz; the tenth, a chrysoprasus; the eleventh, a jacinth; the twelfth, an amethyst.

One can research the details and original meanings of each stone, or one can just grasp the general picture of a foundation far more beautiful than anything adorning the counterfeit religion of the whore of Babylon.

Revelation 21:21 And the twelve gates were twelve pearls: every several gate was of one pearl: and the street of the city was pure gold, as it were transparent glass.

This reveals that our home in eternity will be fabulous.

Revelation 21:22 And I saw no temple therein: for the Lord God Almighty and the Lamb are the temple of it.

Local churches from our world will be united and absorbed into the heavenly congregation. We who are united with God, are also part of that temple (1 Corinthians 3:16-17; 2 Corinthians 6:16)

Revelation 21:23 And the city had no need of the sun, neither of the moon, to shine in it: for the glory of God did lighten it, and the Lamb is the light thereof.

A brightness that we cannot see while in this earthly body will be visible when in our heavenly body.

Revelation 21:24 And the nations of them which are saved shall walk in the light of it: and the kings of the earth do bring their glory and honour into it.

A precursor to this is found in the prophecy of Isaiah 60:3-14. There will still be kings and nations in eternity (Revelation 2:26-27).

Revelation 21:25 And the gates of it shall not be shut at all by day: for there shall be no night there.

There will be no need for the shutting of gates, for the holy nations are welcome and there is perfect security. Eternally rejuvenated, there is no need for bodily rest, but eternal rest (Hebrews 3-4), in a different manner to our rhythm of daily physical rest on earth. There is peace and safety and no spiritual darkness, no heresy, calamity or distress.

Revelation 21:26 And they shall bring the glory and honour of the nations into it.

What greater gift can any nation among the redeemed offer but themselves to God!

Revelation 21:27 And there shall in no wise enter into it any thing that defileth, neither whatsoever worketh abomination, or maketh a lie: but they which are written in the Lamb's book of life.

Where only those made holy live, nothing unclean or unholy will be. Where only those who smell good to God will live, no immoral stench will exist. Where only truth exists, no falsehood can be found. David was inspired to write, "all men are liars" (Psalm 116:11). Yet, with repentance, confession, and forgiveness is life forever in Jesus.

This present earth is filled with corruption of every kind, but there will be a new heaven, new earth and new Jerusalem where peace and rest from all evil will last forever.

Revelation 22 - the River of Life

Let's now look at the joyful conclusion of all things, pictured in a pure river of water of life, and the tree of life, access to which will be regained. We also read the last written words of Jesus, "Surely I am coming quickly." All this is recorded in Revelation 22.

Revelation 22:1 And he shewed me a pure river of water of life, clear as crystal, proceeding out of the throne of God and of the Lamb.

This is reminiscent of the inspired words written by several ancient prophets (Isaiah 35; Ezekiel 47; Zechariah 14). The water of life is pictured in the rivers springing from the garden, the water from the rock which Moses struck, prophecies of streams in the desert, and the living water that Jesus promised (John 7:38).

Revelation 22:2 In the midst of the street of it, and on either side of the river, was there the tree of life, which bare twelve manner of fruits, and yielded her fruit every month: and the leaves of the tree were for the healing of the nations.

Access to the tree of life is restored.

Revelation 22:3 And there shall be no more curse: but the throne of God and of the Lamb shall be in it; and his servants shall serve him:

The curse which began at Eden will be over (Zechariah 14:11).

Revelation 22:4 And they shall see his face; and his name shall be in their foreheads.

This is the diametric opposite of the mark of the beast, the name of God, which will be in their foreheads, in their thoughts.

Revelation 22:5 And there shall be no night there; and they need no candle, neither light of the sun; for the Lord God giveth them light: and they shall reign for ever and ever.

Whereas before we knew that the light was on the city. Here it is on them.

Revelation 22:6 And he said unto me, These sayings are faithful and true: and the Lord God of the holy prophets sent his angel to shew unto his servants the things which must shortly be done.

When we read the word "shortly" we must understand that God counts time differently to us.

Revelation 22:7 Behold, I come quickly: blessed is he that keepeth the sayings of the prophecy of this book.

How quickly? It will come quicker than expected. Why do we keep the sayings? While many may be tempted to avoid Revelation because of its mystery and frequent misuse in wild speculation, keeping these words in observation and memory is a blessing. It symbolically reveals the victory of Jesus and His saints over all evil.

Revelation 22:8 And I John saw these things, and heard them. And when I had heard and seen, I fell down to worship before the feet of the angel which shewed me these things.

John was once before rebuked for doing this (Revelation 19:10) where he previously specifically worshipped the angel. Here he seems to be worshipping God in front of the angel's feet, but still it is too close to idolatry for comfort.

Revelation 22:9 Then saith he unto me, See thou do it not: for I am thy fellowservant, and of thy brethren the prophets, and of them which keep the sayings of this book: worship God.

If we have ever had any doubts about bowing down before the saints of history, this angel teaches us a valuable lesson.

Revelation 22:10 And he saith unto me, Seal not the sayings of the prophecy of this book: for the time is at hand.

However long the gospel age may continue, it is the end. Whereas the words of Daniel were sealed until the end (Daniel 12:4, 9), these words are for the end. The time is at hand for this sequence of prophetic events to be fulfilled. Though they are a continuity of evils existing in ancient empires, they will culminate in heaven's victory.

Revelation 22:11 He that is unjust, let him be unjust still: and he which is filthy, let him be filthy still: and he that is righteous, let him be righteous still: and he that is holy, let him be holy still.

For those of us that are concerned about immorality in the world and heresy and apostasy within the church, these words are exactly what we need. Let it be! Let people choose and so be it.

Revelation 22:12 And, behold, I come quickly; and my reward is with me, to give every man according as his work shall be.

Though salvation is a free gift, we show our faith by our works and the size of our reward depends on what we do (Isaiah 40:10; 62:11).

Revelation 22:13 I am Alpha and Omega, the beginning and the end, the first and the last.

Jesus Christ is God plain and simple.

Revelation 22:14 Blessed are they that do his commandments, that they may have right to the tree of life, and may enter in through the gates into the city.

This literally says, "Blessed are they that wash their robes." How are they washed? They are washed in the blood of the Lamb (Revelation 7:14). This is the last beatitude spoken by Jesus, after a long list of beatitudes throughout His earthly ministry.

Revelation 22:15 For without are dogs, and sorcerers, and whoremongers, and murderers, and idolaters, and whosoever loveth and maketh a lie.

Dogs may picture spiritual predators. Sorcerers used drugs and magic. Next refers to anyone who practices sexual immorality. Any kind of murderer is meant, of the born, unborn, through poisoned food, reckless driving, pollution or any other kind of disregard for human life. Idolatry is the worship of any kind of false god, serving images, money or materialism. The last of these is intentional and conscious love of falsehoods.

Revelation 22:16 I Jesus have sent mine angel to testify unto you these things in the churches. I am the root and the offspring of David, and the bright and morning star.

The words "root and offspring" refer to Jesus being before David as the Lord God and also his descendant. The morning star pictures the beginning of a new day after a long, dark night for all humanity. The original Greek omits "and" simply saying "the offspring of David, the bright morning star."

Revelation 22:17 And the Spirit and the bride say, Come. And let him that heareth say, Come. And let him that is athirst come. And whosoever will, let him take the water of life freely.

Deep understanding of all the mysteries takes a lifetime, but the invitation from the Spirit and the Church is open. All who hear pass on the invitation. Those who are thirsty and willing are invited.

Revelation 22:18 For I testify unto every man that heareth the words of the prophecy of this book, If any man shall add unto these things, God shall add unto him the plagues that are written in this book:

Verbal or written commentary is not adding in this sense, but following the example of those who "helped the people to understand … So they read distinctly from the book, in the Law of God; and they gave the sense, and helped them to understand the reading" (Nehemiah 8:7-8 NKJV). It is dangerous to add man-made rules about vain traditions and fads not taught by Christ, the apostles and prophets, and all churches have been guilty of this. May God have mercy on us.

Revelation 22:19 And if any man shall take away from the words of the book of this prophecy, God shall take away his part out of the book of life, and out of the holy city, and from the things which are written in this book.

Treating the book of Revelation or any part of the Bible like a menu, where we pick and choose only those parts that we like, and ignore or delete those parts we don't like, is just as bad as adding dogmas not taught by the Scriptures.

Revelation 22:20 He which testifieth these things saith, Surely I come quickly. Amen. Even so, come, Lord Jesus.

The true Christian looks forward in great joy to receive Jesus now and at His second coming.

Revelation 22:21 The grace of our Lord Jesus Christ be with you all. Amen.

May the kindness and favor of our Lord be with us all. Amen!

In this chapter, we have seen a vision of the joyful conclusion of all things, a river of the water of life, and access to the tree of life regained. May our Lord come quickly and show us His grace!

In this book of Revelation, we have seen the mysteries of Christ revealed in symbolism that shows the end of all evil and the dawning of a new time of supreme joy. May He come quickly! May He grant us that blessed eternal life contained in these prophecies!

Versions of the Bible Used

KJV Unless otherwise stated, all quotes are from the King James Bible. Public Domain.

NKJV New King James Version (NKJV) Scripture taken from the New King James Version®. Copyright © 1982 by Thomas Nelson. Used by permission. All rights reserved.

NIV Holy Bible, New International Version®, NIV® Copyright © 1973, 1978, 1984, 2011 by Biblica, Inc.® Used by permission. All rights reserved worldwide.

NLT Scripture quotations are taken from the Holy Bible, New Living Translation, copyright ©1996, 2004, 2007.Used by permission of Tyndale House Publishers, Inc., Carol Stream, Illinois 60188. All Rights Reserved.

ESV The ESV® Bible (The Holy Bible, English Standard Version®) copyright © 2001 by Crossway Bibles, a publishing ministry of Good News Publishers. The ESV® text has been reproduced in cooperation with and by permission of Good News Publishers. Unauthorized reproduction of this publication is prohibited. All rights reserved. The ESV® Bible (The Holy Bible, English Standard Version®) is adapted from the Revised Standard Version of the Bible, copyright Division of Christian Education of the National Council of the Churches of Christ in the U.S.A. All rights reserved.

NASB New American Standard Bible Copyright © 1960, 1962, 1963, 1968, 1971, 1972, 1973, 1975, 1977, 1995 by The Lockman Foundation, La Habra, Calif. All rights reserved. For Permission to Quote Information visit http://www.lockman.org

HCSB Holman Christian Standard Bible®, Copyright © 1999, 2000, 2002, 2003, 2009 by Holman Bible Publishers. Used by permission.

ISV The Holy Bible: International Standard Version® Release 2.1 Copyright © 1996-2012 The ISV Foundation ALL RIGHTS RESERVED INTERNATIONALLY.

NET Bible copyright © 1996-2006 by Biblical Studies Press, L.L.C. http://netbible.com. Used by permission. All rights reserved.

Webster Bible, 1883. Public Domain.

The World English Bible. Public Domain.

References

Gregg, Steve. *Revelation Four Views: A Parallel Commentary.* 1997. Thomas Nelson, Inc. Nashville, Tennessee.

www.ingramcontent.com/pod-product-compliance
Lightning Source LLC
Chambersburg PA
CBHW071618150726
48000CB00004B/1785